FOUR WAY BARGELLO

Dorothy Kaestner

Photos by George S. Kaestner

Charles Scribner's Sons • New York

Printed in the United States of America
Library of Congress Catalog Card Number 77-39335
SBN 684-12912-4 (trade cloth)

Design by PAT SMYTHE

Acknowledgements

My thanks to Mrs. H. Weller Keever, Mrs. Harold Jockers, Mrs. Charles Fagg, Mrs. Samuel F. Pierson, Mrs. O. K. Myers and Mrs. Richard Sanders for allowing me to illustrate their pieces, to Mrs. George C. Park, Mrs. Walter Hafner and to Mrs. Sanders for helping me to work some of my designs, and to Marcia Simmons and her friend Mrs. Deane Benson for allowing me to use Mrs. Benson's old Bargello design. My thanks also to my editor, Elinor Parker.

Dedication

To my husband for his patience and his labors in blocking and photographing the designs so many times.

Contents

Color Plates

Publisher's Note

It has not been possible to reproduce every pattern in full color. However, the author's combinations of color are so interesting that we have included them in every case, even when the illustration is only in half tone.

Four Way Bargello

Foreword

This book has come to be because I became interested, first in Bargello, then in the exploration of working it in four directions. The more I explored, the more interested I became.

My first piece of four-way Bargello was started approximately ten years ago. I placed a mirror on a Bargello design drawn on graph paper in a way that showed me how it would look if I mitered a corner. This intrigued me so much that I graphed a design starting in the center and mitering the four corners. From this idea, I started a piece on canvas and then put it aside and forgot it until late winter 1970.

Going through some of my unfinished needlework one day, I ran across the forgotten piece and since Bargello had become so popular, I was really inspired to work out other patterns. These came about by playing with line arrangements on graph paper until something looked good and then actually working on the canvas; I graphed only enough of the design to get me started, then did the rest of the designing as I stitched. As the work progressed, the corners would actually surprise me because they grew and looked so different. These corners were a bit difficult in the beginning, but as I did more and more designs they became easy.

After 4 or 5 designs were in various stages of completion, one of my customers, Mrs. Richard Sanders, became inquisitive and excited by them and offered to complete some so that she could learn how to do them. She became so excited with this way of doing Bargello that she designed several pieces herself and was kind enough to allow me to include them in this book.

I had a faint idea of putting my designs in a book so I showed the designs to a couple of the book salesmen. They thought that they were so different they pushed me to go ahead. This gave me the courage to show them to my present editor at Scribner's. When she showed great interest in them I became really enthusiastic about doing it. Once the decision was made to write the book, I felt that it should show the use of more contemporary color combinations as well as a different way of working Bargello.

As a handweaver, I studied color and texture with Jack Lenor Larsen, color theory with the late Jackie Von Ladau and basic design with Professor Matthew Wysocki. I love using color and mixing together colors that others would shudder at until they see them worked. You will see that I combine colors of different "families," meaning that I combine a few shades of one color with some shades of another closely related color. One of my favorite ways of using color is analogous—that is, to use 3 colors that are side by side on the color wheel: for example, blue, blue-green, green—orange-red, red, blue-red, etc. When you use analogous colors there is always a relationship among them. This is a rule which should help those of you who are afraid to choose your own color schemes. Look at the color wheel and you will see what I mean.

Introduction

Anyone who has worked Bargello knows that all the stitches go in one direction—vertical. I have seen only a few pieces where some stitches are horizontal as well as vertical and mitered at the corners. I am not the inventor of this method of working, but I do feel that no one has explored it to any length before.

Bargello has the advantage of working up very quickly as compared to regular tent stitch. However, I like to combine the two at times, especially in the four way method. Bargello is geometric in design rather than pictorial, although I have managed a few exceptions—ribbon candy—peacock feathers—tulips. You are really working with shape, direction and color.

This book will show you various ways a design can be used:—by using only part of a design—shading the same design in various ways—using different color combinations—making a square or a rectangle—using it as an outer border or as a center motif—as a repeat pattern. And, of course, there is no reason why most of these designs couldn't be worked in the conventional way, that is, in one direction only. The rectangular pieces readily show you this.

If you intend to do several matching pieces of any counted needlepoint, be sure to buy all your canvas from the same roll. The count of the canvas will vary very slightly from one roll to another. I have also found that most people cannot remember if they bought 12, 13 or 14 mesh canvas before and invariably get the wrong one. They discover the mistake after the work is finished and it turns out to be a different size. Tag any unused pieces of canvas with the mesh size before storing them.

These designs have been worked on varying mono canvases. I used mesh counts 10, 12, 13, 14, 16 and 18. With Persian yarn use the 3 strands that cling together on the 12, 13 or 14 canvas. Use 4 and sometimes 5 strands on the 10 canvas and 2 strands on the 16 and 18 mesh. When doing tent stitch you will probably use fewer number of strands than for Bargello.

Mesh Size	Bargello	Tent Stitch
10	4 or 5 strands	3 strands
12	3 "	2 or 3 "
13 and 14	3 "	2 "
*16	2 "	1 "
18	2 "	1 "

A word of caution: in working Bargello, it is very easy to pull the yarn too tight, thus shortening your yarn and allowing the canvas to show through. When working in 4 directions the canvas can become quite warped. Pull your yarn so that the stitch lies flat, neither too loose nor too tight. The Persian yarn varies occasionally in thickness. Sometimes I find a color is thin enough so that I have to add another strand. This is probably caused by dyes, the darker shades tending to be thinner than the lighter ones.

Designs are all around us—books, magazines and mostly nature. In every beautiful picture I see of nature, birds—flowers—trees—seascapes—landscapes, I see designs and colors. Where can one find more beautiful colors and color combinations than in nature?

In spring we see lovely yellow greens in the trees when the leaves are starting to open. Then, some of them are assorted reds and pinks. These colors are on the deciduous trees. But among them will be the evergreen trees and shrubs with their blue-green or bronze-green or gray-green. This, then, suggests to me that greens are nature's neutrals. They go with all her colors. Neither is she afraid to mix them. This is one thing an artist learns—to get several kinds of green in a painting, not just several shades of one green. Of course there are times when we only want one green or one color for a particular reason. I'm only trying to emphasize that you *can* mix them. Too many people are afraid of color.

When planning some color schemes, I try to use bright and dull, light and dark—this gives me contrast.

Another thing to remember with color—yellow is a forward color, purple a receding color. Yellows and reds are "hot" colors, blues and blue-greens are "cool" colors. We can work with all hot, all cool, or cool with an accent of hot, or hot with an accent of cool.

*Nantucket yarn		
16 mesh	4 strands	2 strands

I think more and more people are becoming aware of how lovely the analogous colorings are. I used to hear, "Those colors swear at each other." They don't swear, they sing and sparkle. Another way to make color sparkle is to mix a strand of red with orange red, or with blue red. So long as the colors are of the same value they seem to melt into a richer color.

Using tapestry yarn

Tapestry yarn comes in several ways, usually as 7½ yard small skeins, 20 yard cards, 40 yard (1 oz. skeins) 2 oz. skeins and 4 oz. skeins.

The 1 oz, 2 oz., and 4 oz. skeins should be untwisted so that they can be cut. The 1 oz. skeins should be cut only once for a comfortable working length. The 2 oz. and 4 oz. skeins are cut in half again, which gives you approximately ¾ yard.

When using the small skeins or cards, cut off a length at a time except when splitting the yarn. Then cut two identical lengths at a time. If you are using only two strands, your third strand of each length will match without waste.

For rugs where five or more strands are used, cut the larger skeins only once. In working the larger stitches, the yarn does not get pulled through the canvas so many times, therefore it doesn't get the wear of the smaller canvases. It also gets used up much faster.

Working Tent Stitch (basket weave)

One thing to remember is that the needle always comes up in the lower left and goes down in the upper right of the stitch.

At the top of photo on page 6 I have replaced the weft or horizontal threads of the canvas with some colored threads so as to show the difference between the horizontal (dark) threads and the vertical (white) threads.

To get evener stitching and also to cover the canvas better, stitch over the horizontal threads (which are on top of the vertical thread), on the up rows (left ex.) and over the vertical threads (which are the top threads now), on the down rows (right ex.). Also notice that the needle, as it goes in and out of the canvas, runs parallel to the horizontal thread of the canvas as you work up and parallel to the vertical thread as you work down.

In the next example, I used a light colored yarn on the up rows and a dark yarn on the down rows. This shows that when you have completed an up row with a stitch at the top—in order to start a down row another stitch must be placed at the top beside it. Also, when you finish a down row with a stitch at the bottom and all the way out to the edge—in order to start an up row you must place another stitch below the last one.

The lower example shows how the needle is inserted into the canvas when working bargello. As you work up, left ex., and as you work down, right ex. This is the economical method of working and has less yarn on the back. I have worked all my pieces in this manner.

Working Bargello

The basic 4-2 step of Bargello stitch is straight up over 4 horizontal threads of the canvas, then dropping back 2 threads next to the preceding stitch. You can go up or down in this manner either one stitch on each step, or 2 or more stitches on each of the steps. As you add more stitches to a step or subtract, the slant of the design will change. You can make it steep or spread it out. See chart on next page.

Bargello can be done in a 2-1 step, 3-1, 4-1, 4-2, 5-1, 5-2, 6-1, 6-2, etc. I am using the name Bargello loosely because the long step and short step in combination is often referred to as Hungarian Point. I have worked most of these designs in the 4-2 step. There are some variations. In the blue and turquoise Kaleidoscope (page 25), I worked some rows in a 4-2 step and some in a 3-1 step. Not all designs can be worked in various size steps. I tried to work a diamond with a 6-1 step and it wouldn't work. To make an even diamond, your step back has to be 1/2 the length of the stitch: for example, 4-2, 6-3, etc.

When working from graph paper, each square of the paper represents a horizontal *thread* of the canvas. The vertical *lines* of the paper represent the vertical *threads* of the canvas. See chart showing the marked-off graph paper and photo showing the marked-off canvas (pages 8 and 9).

Before working on your canvas, find the center hole (you do this by measuring or by counting), and mark it, preferably with a laundry marking pen or a Studio fine line magic marker. Do not make too heavy a line, just dark enough to see it. Now, mark the miter lines on your canvas as shown in diagram 1. This is very important so that you know when you are at a corner. In marking the canvas diagonally, the lines should touch at each intersection of the threads as shown. If you wish to mark off the rows of stitches you can just put small marks up and down and across the center stitches as shown. This acts as a check point for you as you work.

When working four way Bargello, the stitch length will vary at the miter. Diagram 2 shows a 4-2 step V pattern. The stitches next to the 4 center stitches leave a single square of the graph (or a single thread of the canvas) at the miter lines. The next stitches leave 2 squares or threads, then 3, then 4, then 5. When I come to where there are 5 threads I prefer to work over

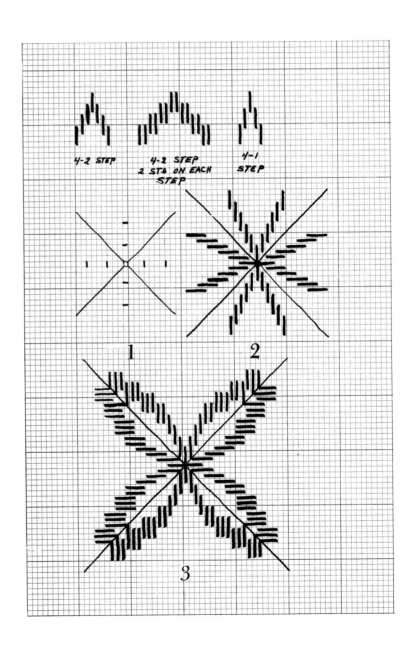

all of them. Instead of leaving that 1 square or thread on those stitches next to the center, I would have made that stitch go to the corner miter like the ones in diagram 3. I prefer not to leave a single thread stitch because it seems to sink and does not look well. However, I have been trapped into it at times.

The corners of diagram 3 shows how you would miter when you have several stitches on the same step. The tops of the stitches remain even, but they become shorter at the miter.

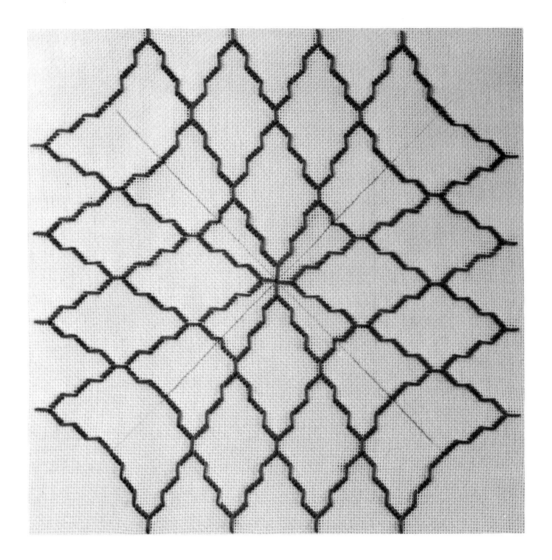

When starting a pattern, work the design in all four directions, not just in one quarter section. This way you can soon start connecting at the corners so that you can work each row all the way around.

If there is a dominant outline of motifs, it is easier to set up the pattern by doing all of the outline first as shown in the above photo. Then work one color at a time. Under artificial light it is sometimes difficult to see the difference between close shades, so if you pull one shade and follow the whole design filling in where that shade belongs it helps to avoid errors.

I have heard people refer to a right and wrong direction of using needlepoint canvas, but in working four way Bargello we naturally have to disregard this. I usually disregard it anyway. However, I do like using Maggie Lane's method of working the tent stitch—working over the horizontal thread of the canvas weave on the up rows and over the vertical thread of the canvas weave on the down rows. (See *Needlepoint by Design.*) You will find that the canvas is never really square so that your finished design will be a trifle longer than wide. A few extra rows of background on the short sides will not be noticed.

To digress—one day in our store I was standing around, being available to the many customers just sort of looking, at the moment, but also asking for information. I was working out the four way leaf stitch design. (I often go on stitching while waiting for customers to decide on what they want.) This leaf stitch was giving me a bit of a problem getting the count right and deciding how I would turn the corner. One woman wanted to see what I was doing and became interested in the four direction idea. Then she asked, "Do you ever make a mistake?" I assured her that I certainly did. The rest of the afternoon I did nothing but make mistakes. Please, don't feel ashamed of making mistakes so long as you're willing to correct them. Too many people are afraid to start anything for fear of making an error and being ridiculed for it. We all make mistakes and learn by them. Some of our so-called mistakes become new ideas.

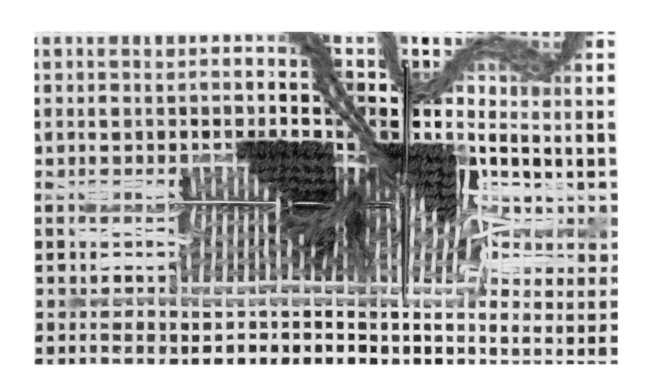

Needle Points

1. When cutting canvas for a given project be sure to leave 1½″ to 2″ extra canvas on all edges. Try not to work to the very edge.

2. It is better to machine stitch a hem on the edges of your canvas than to use masking tape. The reason for this is that when the worked piece is blocked, the hemmed edges are stronger for pulling and nailing. The needlepoint needs to be dampened so as to make it easier to pull it square and this makes masking tape gummy. Also, canvases with no hems fray apart at the edges while you are working and become very difficult to block.

3. While you are working your needlepoint be sure to run all ends about an inch under the stitches on the wrong side and cut off the excess. I've seen some pieces brought in for blocking that looked like a shaggy rug on the wrong side. Unless this is all trimmed off the finished piece will always be lumpy. It pays to be neat in your work.

4. If you notice that you are going to need more yarn to complete a project, do not use up all that you have before matching it to more. Leave at least 6 strands. It is easier to match color by having the pieces of yarn in your hand rather than stitched into the work. The color does look different when you see it as little stitches. Of course, it is best to have a label with color number and dye lot, but if a dye lot is gone the color may be slightly different. Then, by having these strands of yarn you can blend the new lot in. One way to blend is to use a strand of the old and a strand of the new together until the old is used up. Another way is to alternate rows—one of the new, then one of the old until the old is gone. Of course, it is always best to have more than enough yarn to begin with, especially for your background.

The Patterns

Numbers refer to Paternayan colors unless otherwise specified.

Pages 14-15 show 7 variations of a random pattern. Page 14, row 1 shows a 2-1 step—row 2 a 3-1 step—row 3 a 4-2 step and row 4 a 4-1 step. Page 15, row 1 shows a 5-1 step—row 2 a 5-2 step and row 3 a 6-1 step. You can see how shallow the 2-1 step is and how deep the pattern becomes in the 6-1 step. Chart below shows the 4-2 step.

In working four way Bargello some designs can be varied by changing the step from the usual 4-2 step to a shorter or a longer stitch. When changing to another length of stitch the design will change considerably. The corners or miters will be very different.

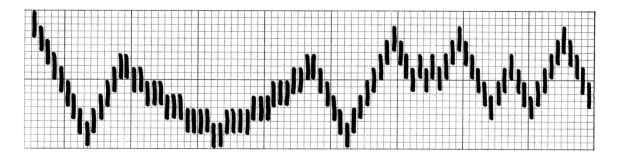

In the turquoise design on Plate 1 I've taken a section of the pattern on page 15 with a 6-1 step. I started with the bright turquoise No. 738 at the middle and set up the pattern repeat around. As I got to my 5th shade another (almost) repeat was able to fit the corners. It took 6 rows to make a square of just over 11″ on 12 mesh canvas. Dark turquoise 750, medium turquoise 755, aqua, dark to light 783, 793, 765. See chart on page 15.

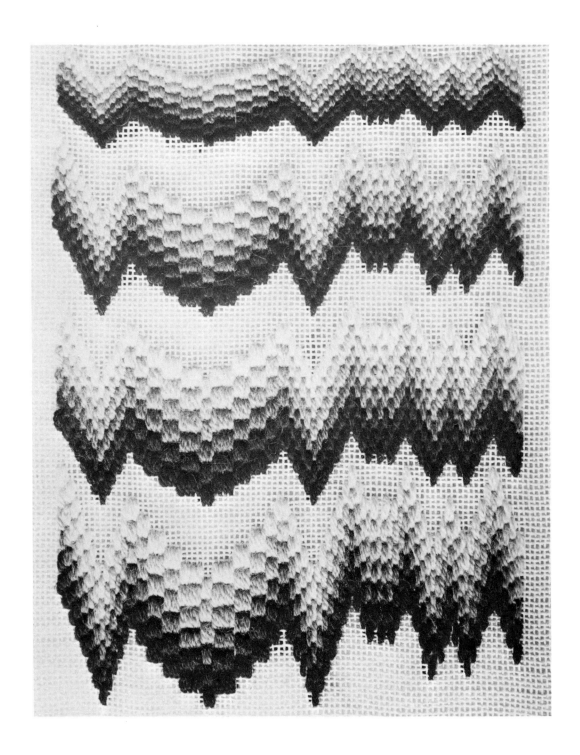

In the orange rendition on Plate 1 I used the 4-2 step and the same section of the pattern. This time I started with the lightest shade at the center. It took 16 rows to make the same size square as the turquoise piece; notice how different the design appears. Persian colors dark to light are 242, 958, 968, 978, 988, 454.

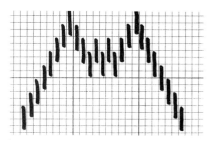

1

2

3

Blue green 6-2 step

Blue and green 6-2 step square This is not too different from the turquoise except that by using 2 color groups the design does change. Some of the other patterns would work this way too. 12 mesh 3 strands. Persian colors. Blue dark to light 723, 731, 733, 741, 743, B43. Greens dark to light 510, 555, 570, 575. See Plate 1.

Orange 4-2 step

Turquoise 6-1 step

Spanish tiles, Mediterranean colors, regular Bargello

I designed this piece some years ago and put it aside. In May, 1970, after being in Spain, I picked it up and it immediately suggested Spain and the Mediterranean Sea. I wasn't even thinking of anything Spanish at the time I designed it. The colors are dark blue 723, dark turquoise 750, green 524, medium turquoise 755, medium light turquoise 760, light turquoise 765, white 005. 14 mesh, 3 strands, Persian yarn, 4-2 step. See Plate 2.

This again shows how to take a regular Bargello design and turn it into four way Bargello. Notice the center motif. This would be very effective as a repeat design. I would suggest filling the vacant spaces between motifs with tent stitch. 12 mesh, 3 strands, Persian colors, dark copper 414, burnt orange 427, 440, 441, yellows 442, 437, 438.

The chart on page 20 shows two other ways of using the Spanish tile motif, using the center motif of the four way design and repeating it. This shows the joined tiles shaded from the outside toward the center, A. The other version, B, keeps the sides of the tiles separated and each group of four shades from the dark at the central point toward light at the outside— but these outside points also meet with three other outside points, which if considered a group of four, shades from light at the central points toward dark at the outside points. The chart indicates just enough to give the idea.

Spanish tiles, sun colors, four way Bargello

This was the first four way Bargello that I started, then put aside for so long. I finally finished it. Once I got started again on this method of working I became so excited about it that I couldn't stop. In this piece the basic diamonds remained the same. They changed only at the corners. Persian yarn colors, 14 mesh, 3 strands. Red, dark to light 845, 850, 860, 865. Purple-red, dark to light 221, 821, 827. Dark green 524, light green 534. See Photo on page 21. Chart below shows where to place the colors. Then they just keep repeating themselves.

Reds and greens

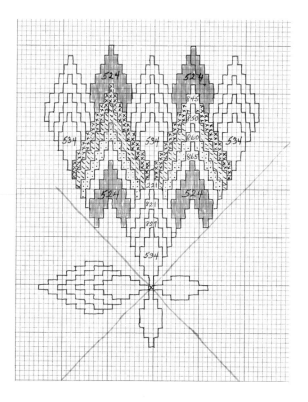

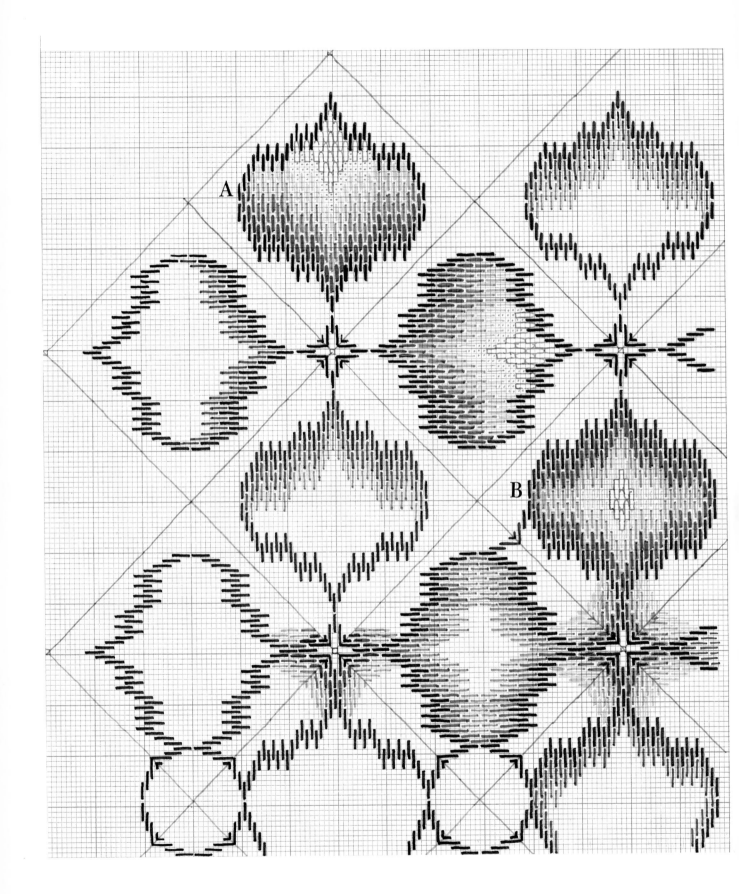

Reds and greens

Red-orange to yellow undulations

This is a very simple one to do. I just set up an undulating pattern and followed through with the sequence of colors as follows: starting with the dark red-orange 956, 968, 978, 988, orange 960, 970, 975, gold 427, 447, 457, yellow 580, 468. This is a good example of blending one family of colors into the next family—or moving around the color wheel. Persian yarns, 14 mesh, 3 strands. See Plate 4.

Photo below shows a variation of this that Mrs. H. Keever of New Canaan did in greens as slippers for her husband. From the center point straight up and down and across she flipped the design over—just reversing the pattern. Persian colors, 18 mesh, 2 strands. Yellow-green, light to dark G54, G64, 574, G74, blue-green 524, 526, 534, 536, G37, yellow 545, 550, 565.

I lent her my original design over a weekend so she could copy the pattern and when her husband saw it, he requested a 5 foot square copy for his office.

Red and orange points and diamonds

I started with the four little diamonds in the center and let the surrounding ones grow as as I progressed, in fact I let the design continue all the way to the edge. The design could have been stopped at several points and another stitch used to complete the canvas. The lower photo on facing page shows a part of the design as a complete design in itself. The upper photo shows outline partly filled in for various stopping points which in themselves are complete designs. Persian colors, 14 mesh, 3 strands. Reds dark to light R50, R60, R70, 860, 831, oranges 958, 968, 978, 988, 454. Color plate 3.

Green leaves   This is rather tricky. I divided my canvas in four—up and down and across, instead of diagonally. I made a diagram on graph paper first, then counted it onto the canvas. Half of each leaf is worked in one direction and the other half is worked in the opposite direction, working from the outside of each leaf toward the center. The background was worked in an opposing direction to each leaf half. Even though I counted from the graph paper, I evidently miscounted a little and some of the leaves vary, but I don't think that this spoils the design. Persian colors, 14 mesh, 3 strands. Yellow-green leaves, starting from dark to light G64, 574, G74, 592. The other green, dark to light 559, 569, 579, 589, G37. The background is 032.

This was started a little out from the center and was worked round and round. The first row was a 4-2 step, the next 2 rows were 3-1 step, the dark turquoise row was a 4-2 step, the next 2 rows were 3-1 step, and I repeated this for the next 6 rows. From there on, I used only the 4-2 step. The tent stitch was used to fill in the center and the corner spaces, but the Bargello stitch was used to complete the outer background. Persian yarn, 14 mesh, 3 strands—tent stitch, 2 strands. Blue, dark to light 723, 731, 741. Turquoise 728, 738, 748.

Blue and turquoise kaleidoscope

Chart for kaleidoscope

I did the green trees first, which could be a complete design in itself as shown below, adding another stitch as a background, or the same stitch in another color. Then I filled in the orange trees, which of course look very different. I used the same stitch for my background. Persian yarn, 10 mesh, 4 strands. Green dark to light 505, 3 small skeins, 527, 3 small skeins, 555, 3 small skeins. Orange dark to light 968, 2 skeins, 978, 2 skeins, 988, 2 skeins. Background 870, a peachy pink. See photo on next page.

Green and orange trees

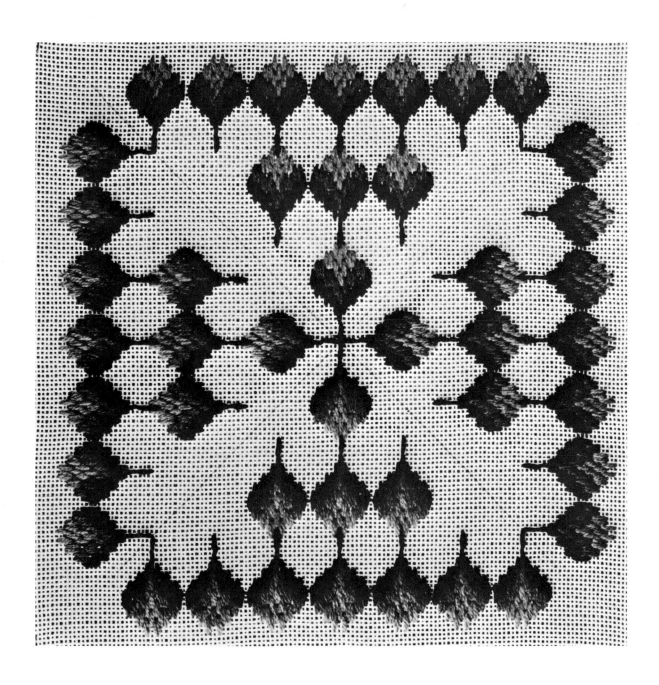

For this design, I didn't start my stitches in the center, but moved up four threads of the canvas (or one stitch). If I had had more room on the canvas I could have made hearts of the design. It's interesting the way it is, but gives ideas for going on further. The canvas is 10 mesh, 5 strands Persian for Bargello, 3 strands for tent stitch. Colors, black 050, dark blue-gray 311, dark gray 180, medium dark gray 182, medium gray 184, light gray 186, off white 011, white 005 background. One of my students used this design for an oval footstool in reds. Her area was large enough to take the design out farther to make it look almost like a dogwood blossom.

Black to white

Blue "Dahlia"   This started at the center and I just worked the petals round and round, filling the mitered corners. I could have stopped anywhere according to the size I wanted, then worked a tent stitch border. I used a dark border to make the petals really stand out in contrast. The design seems to project from the background. See Plate 5. One of my students has made a belt using the center motif, including the corners, but placing the motifs side by side around the belt. Many of the designs can be used in that way. Mrs. Sanders' version of the blue dahlia used a slightly different petal count. Mine is A, and Mrs. Sander's is B in the charts below.

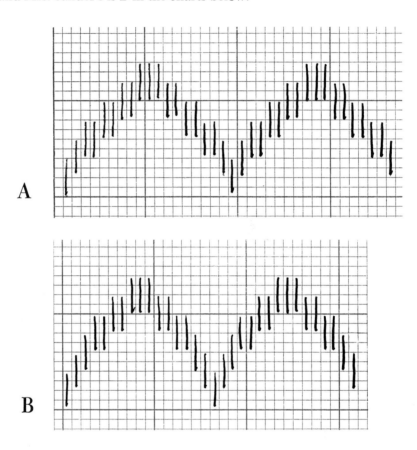

A

B

Copper squares,   Not only did I alternate the direction of the stitch, but I also reversed the
light and dark   shading. One square dark to light, the other light to dark. In the dark squares I have used the stitch vertically and the light squares are done horizontally. 10.mesh—Persian colors dark to light 267, 225, 273, 278, 853, 870. 5 strands for Bargello, 3 strands for tent stitch, Background—green 532. You could use this design differently by making one big square. Starting in the center of the canvas, continue around, repeating the same sequence of shading or reversing the sequence.

Copper squares

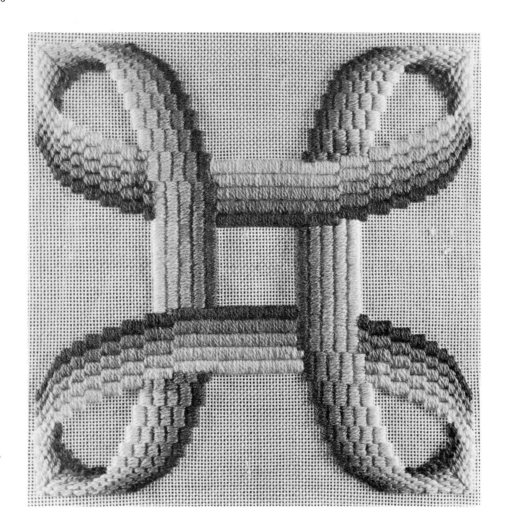

Tiffany pin

Snowflake

After looking through the Tiffany catalogue at Christmas, I thought it would be fun to try working out one of the lovely gold pins. The gold design on turquoise background is the result. This would make a stunning pillow by finishing it as an octagon shape, making the design usable in two directions. Persian colors dark to light 511, 433, 445, 453, 455. Background 718. 14 mesh, 3 strands tent stitch 2 strands. See plate 7.

Tiffany Pin

Someone challenged me to do a snowflake. If you examine snowflake designs, you will see that almost all of them are 6-sided. In four-way Bargello we get either a 4-sided or 8-sided pattern. However, I think that my choice of colors which give an "icy" look and the pattern used do give the impression of a snowflake. 14 mesh, 3 strands. Persian colors dark to light 773, 783, 793, 005. Background 641. See plate 6.

Snowflake

I wanted to try a 6-1, 2-1, 2-1, 2-1, 2-1 arrangement and instead of working a square I wanted a rectangular design suitable for a bench. The shocking pink and lavender blue, shown on next page, developed as a border design. When it came to filling the center, I followed the same pattern and was intrigued by the damask pattern which shows up in the all white background. Persian colors dark pink 827, light pink 828, lavender blue 621, white 005. 14 mesh 3 strands, tent stitch 2 strands.

Shocking pink and lavender blue

After the pink and blue border, I went on to a regular Bargello to try the medallion effect. After setting up my pattern in black, then working 2 rows each side of the first pattern row, I realized I had not copied the design correctly. There is only one peak to the design instead of two peaks, so I have a different pattern. (When working 5 rows of one color in this manner you do have to be careful. I kept getting lost until I counted the remaining spaces left between the peaks so that I would know which side of each line needed another row.) Persian colors, black 050, dark green 545, light green 550, dark orange 970, light orange 975, dark gold 447, light gold 457, 12 mesh, 3 strands. See chart and photo on page 35.

Black, orange yellow and green

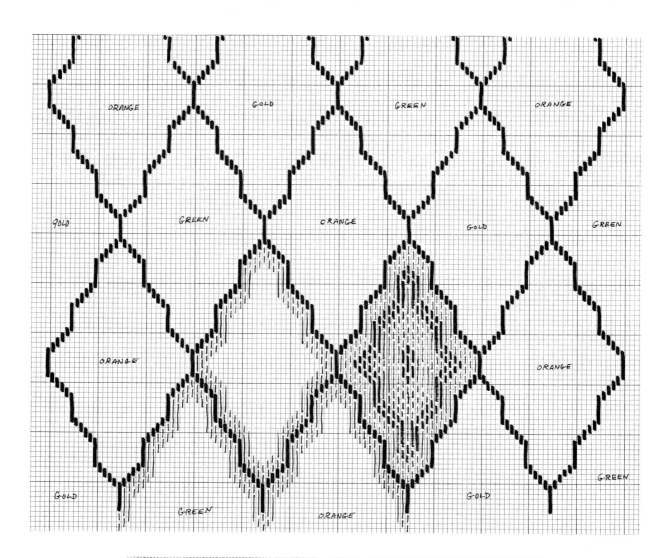

ORANGE GOLD GREEN ORANGE

GOLD GREEN ORANGE GOLD GREEN

ORANGE ORANGE

GREEN

GOLD GREEN ORANGE GOLD

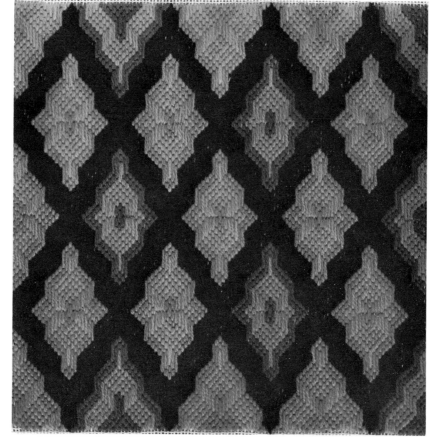

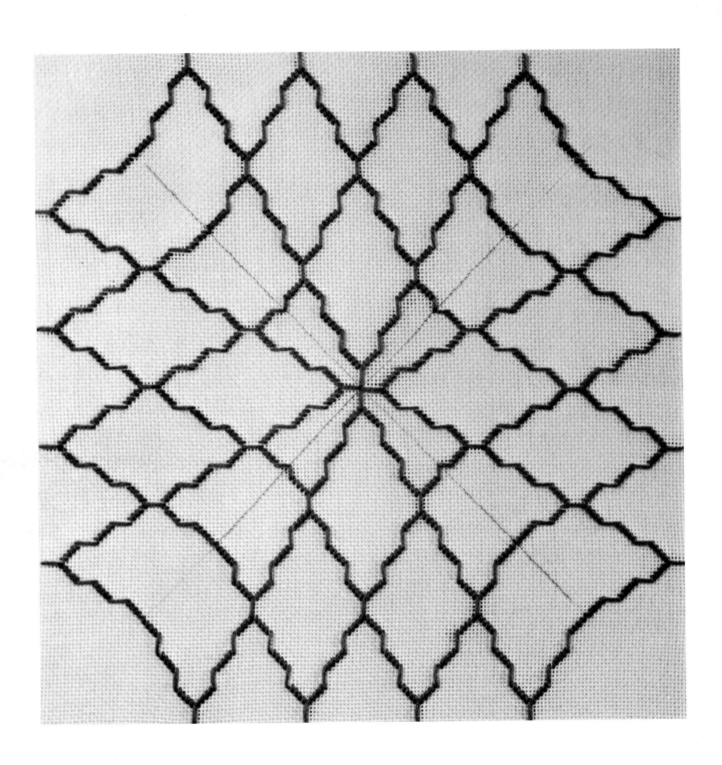

Three blues,
corner cross From the black, orange, yellow and green regular Bargello I went on to
the blue four-way Bargello, using the same single point motif. I again set
up the design with the middle row of medium blue, then worked the two
rows each side of it. By using the light blue to fill in the straight medallions

and the dark blue in the corners, it created a very different effect. 14 mesh Nantucket Needleworks yarn, 4 strands. I should have used 5 strands to cover the canvas better, but this way I think it's easier to see the stitches for copying. Colors, dark to light, 60, 59, 58.

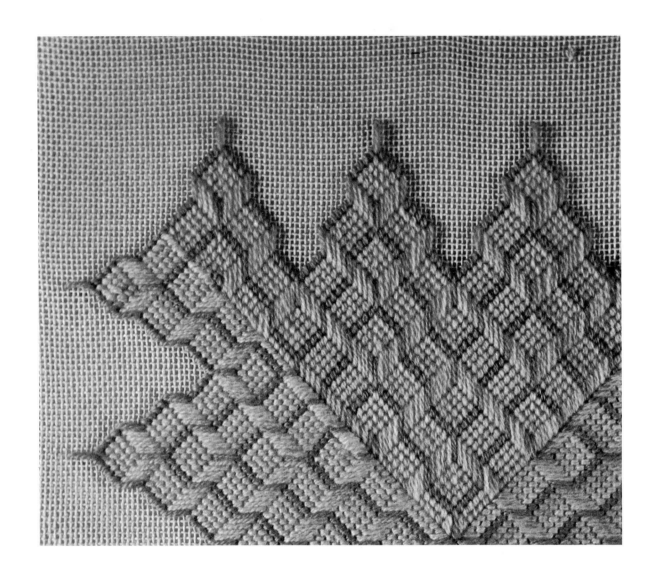

Yellow,
chartreuse   The yellow to chartreuse four-way Bargello square again uses the single point design instead of the double points of the pink and lavender blue. This was started at the center with the chartreuse, then following around with the four shades of yellow dark to light. 12 mesh, Persian 3 strands. Chartreuse 450, yellow dark to light 452, 456, 458, 468. Background 005, tent stitch 2 strands.

After the yellow and chartreuse I worked so that I got a double peak *Orange and pink*
medallion into a square. Counting the center space, I counted 6 spaces *medallion*
up the miter to the right. There I made a long stitch of dark orange and *square*
continued the pattern into a medallion on each of the four sides. I added
two more rows of dark orange inside each medallion. On the corners I have
only one row of dark orange and also reversed the shading. 12 mesh, 3
strands Persian. Dark to light orange 958, 968, 978, 988. Pink R70, 831.
Background 831 following pattern as set up. See plate 8.

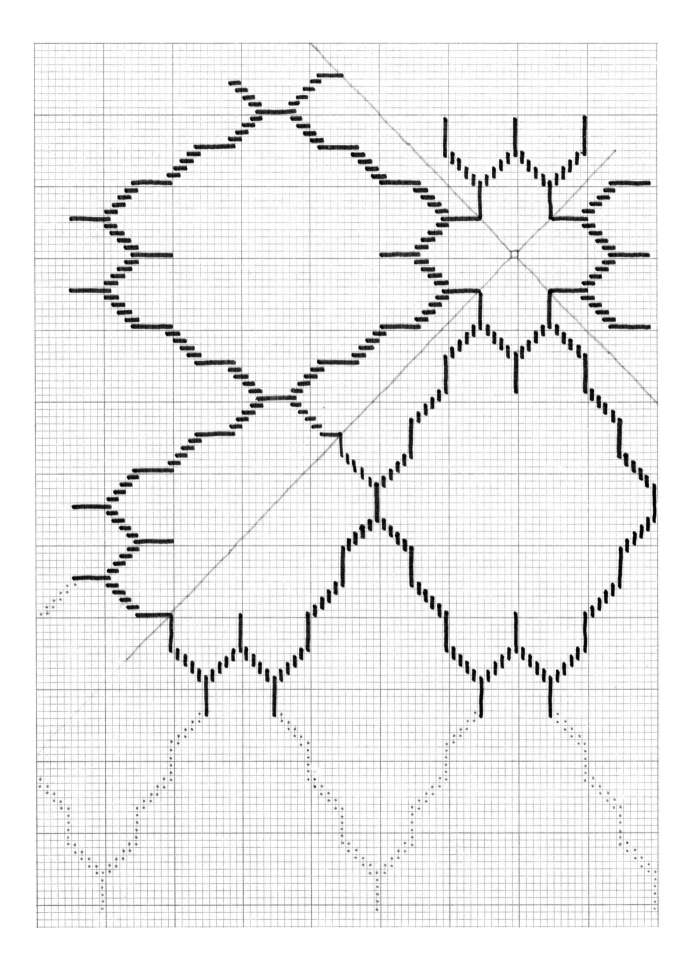

The solid lines in the chart at left give the original outline to set up the design. Then the shading falls within these lines. The dotted lines show how the design can be made larger. If you would like a rectangle, leave out the addition of the corners and extend the design on two sides only.

Brown-rust bench

This design was started by marking a line part way across the center of the canvas, then working the two center rust diamonds. After that, I worked the dark outlines of two motifs to the left and two motifs to the right of the rust diamonds and also placing the other diamonds between the other motifs, then did the three corner diamonds at each end of this row. (To make a longer piece, just add more motifs before working the corner diamonds; to make a shorter piece eliminate some motifs: see the small footstool design, plate 10.) At this point I knew where to place my mitering lines. After marking my four miter lines, I stitched all the dark outlines, working all the way around the center, row after row, until the piece was as large as I wanted. Then I filled in each shade in the same manner. 12 mesh Persian colors. Rust 414, 16 pieces or 2 small skeins; browns, light to dark 014, 29 pieces or 4 small skeins; 138, 23 pieces or 3 small skeins; 132, 23 pieces or 3 small skeins; 126, 18 pieces or 3 small skeins; 116, 23 pieces or 3 small skeins; red-brown outlines 205, 60 pieces or 8 small skeins, using 3 strands. Background 014, following Bargello pattern to edge.

Brown is not one of my favorite colors because I usually feel that it is dull, but by adding the rust and the dark reddish brown, I find that it is more lively. See plate 9.

Small squares

After working the brown rectangular piece, I worked these small squares using the same motif. First of all they look different because of being a square instead of a rectangle—but when the colors are changed and the method of shading is changed you get an entirely different look. It is hard to tell that the motif is still the same. 14 mesh, 3 strands, Persian yarn.

The following photos show the development of this motif. Greens—Outline 504, gray-green dark to light 512, 560, 594, 597, diamonds 574.
Reds—Dark to light 231, 232, 282, 288, 831, diamonds 845
Oranges—Outline 411, burnt orange dark to light 424, 434, 444, 454, diamonds 960.
Blues—Outline 386, dark to light 323, 330, 385, 754, diamonds B43.

Blue

  *Orange*

Red

Green

Blue

Orange

Red

Green

*Blue-green
square*

This piece as shown in plate 10 came next. I like the little diamonds extending beyond the dark outline. They seem to be like ferules or little spike tips on a wrought iron fence. 12 mesh, 3 strands. Persian colors, dark to light 340, 367, 342, 352, 354, 032, diamonds 760.

*Small
blue-green
bench*

This small variation was worked for a small footstool. The bottom photo in plate 10 shows how small the design can be as compared to the brown bench, by just one motif across the center. 12 mesh, 3 strands. Persian colors, dark to light 340, 367, 342, 352, 354. The colors are mostly the same as above, but the method of shading is different. Background 3 strands 342.

*Red small and
large petals*

In this piece I wanted to see if I could make a large motif between the smaller ones. I think it worked out very well. Also, this piece has a more circular effect. The brown canvas is Elsa Williams' Bargello canvas, 13 mesh. She likes this particular canvas for Bargello because she feels that the color shows less and the roughness of it keeps the yarn in place better. It is also less expensive than the white canvases. However, I still use all of them. Persian colors dark to light, 810, 845, 850, 855, 860, 865, 870, 3 strands.

Shocking pink and purple

Shocking pink and purple

The design on the previous page shows how to use just the center motif as a repeat pattern. I used two color combinations to give more color suggestions, but it would be very attractive using only one color combination. If I continued this as a square there would be 4 pink motifs and 5 purple. 13 mesh, Persian colors, 3 strands. Pink dark to light, 644, 645, 649, 659, 828, 831. Purple dark to light, 721, 611, 642, 650, 652, 660. Background, plum 610, 2 strands.

Counting the brown, blue, dark red, orange, green, blue-green square, blue-green bench, red petals, and the pink and purple, there are 9 variations of shading and 10 color combinations. This gives at least 90 possibilities with this one basic motif.

Pink and yellow tulips

Clean pinks and yellows are so pretty together and of course the greens are nice with them. Notice that there are two different kinds of green, following nature's clue.

It will be easier to work from the chart, plate 11, for this design.

14 mesh, 3 strands Persian colors. Dark pink 827, light pink 828, dark green 505, medium green 510, light green 555 on yellow 458. Dark yellow 450, light yellow 458, dark green 520, medium green 527, light green 542 on pink 828.

This design was used for dining room chairs. Since the backs were small and oval, we elongated the vertical tulips. This design could be worked in various ways.

Orange and lettuce green tulips

This is a larger tulip and shows another way of working with them. I really wanted to keep this very fresh with a white background, but the palest yellow tip would not be seen well enough. Against a white background it would need a darker yellow tip. Any of the blue and aqua shades would have been good, but I finally chose the golden-brown 414 as shown. 14 mesh 3 strands Persian. Orange dark to light 960, 965 (Handwork Tapestry's color 128), 442, 437, 040. Green dark to light G64, 574, G74. Background 2 strands.

The chart, plate 12, shows two variations of the corner tulips, without leaves as in worked piece, and with leaves.

Pink and yellow tulips

Orange and lettuce green tulips

I wanted to use some of Nantucket Needleworks' yarns. They have some beautiful colors and the yarn is pleasant to work with. All of the greens except the second darkest is Nantucket yarn. 14 mesh, 4 strands of the Nantucket (as it comes), 3 strands of the Persian. Colors dark to light 78, G64, 84, 83, 82. Background, Persian R70, tent stitch 2 strands. Plate 15 shows how striking the greens are.

Yellow green on bright pink background

Pink evening bag with silver and gold

The chart, plate 13, will be easier to follow for this purse. In the photo it is hard to see the stitches with the metallic yarn and the gusset doesn't show. The gusset design would also make a lovely belt, luggage rack strips, an all-over repeat pattern, or a border.

18 mesh, Camelot silver and gold, Columbia Minerva yarns. Elsa Williams has a gold cloisonné that could also be used. These are used single. Reynolds Yarns has Feu d'artifice which could be used double. There are a number of colors in this yarn. Background, tent stitch single strand Persian yarn. The background color is 860.

In the chart I have diamonds extending beyond the upper and lower outline of the bag shape. Do not include any part of these diamonds for the bag. They are there if you want a square design for something else. The blank squares between the rows of orange (gold) are to be filled in with 2 rows of silver. The gusset strip should be worked 17″ long by 45 canvas threads wide. There are 5 motifs in the strip.

Red outlines with blue greens and yellow greens (Copy of old pattern)

I have been teaching Needlepoint at Silvermine Guild School of The Arts in New Canaan, Connecticut, and one day one of my students brought in an old piece of Bargello belonging to a friend. It was different from any I had seen, so I borrowed it and worked it out in four way Bargello. Plate 16 shows how different it is from the original, as shown at top of facing page. The outline alone as shown would be an interesting design with a solid contrasting background worked either in tent stitch or the Bargello stitch following the pattern of the red. If you examine plate 16, you will see where you can stop at various rounds and have a completed design. 14 mesh canvas, 3 strands Persian. Red 810, pinks dark to light 860, 865, 837, yellow greens dark to light 505, 510, 555, 570, 575, 592, blue greens dark to light 367, 342, 352, 354, 781, 032. It would be interesting to use only one group of greens instead of both groups.

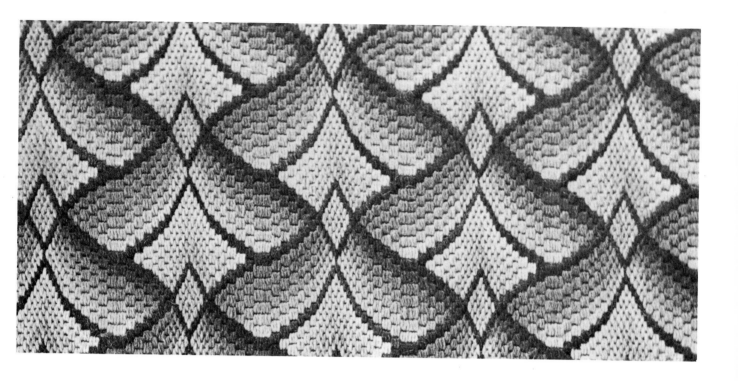

Keever chair seat The rose chair seat was Mrs. Keever's introduction to four way Bargello. She didn't want to repeat the motifs as she worked out from the center so we had consultations on each new row of motifs. Her colors were Persian dark to light. Rose red 236, 232, 282, 288, 831, coral red 810, 850, 855, 860, 865. Background 012. 14 mesh 3 strands, tent stitch 2 strands. See color plate 17.

Plate 1

Plate 2

Plate 3

Plate 4

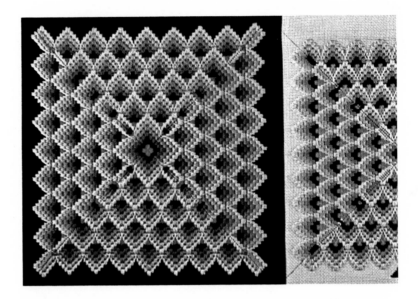

Plate 5

Plate 6

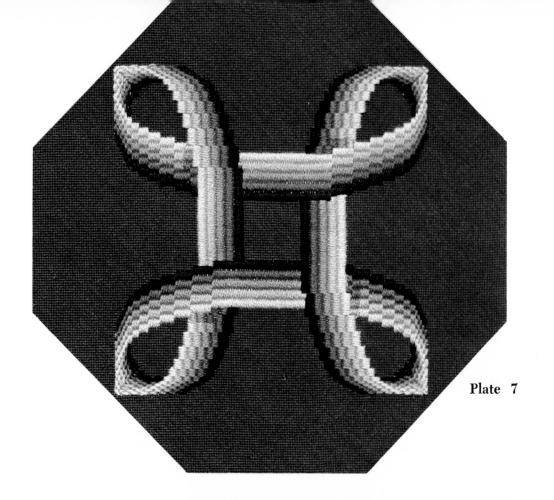

Plate 7

Plate 8

Plate 9

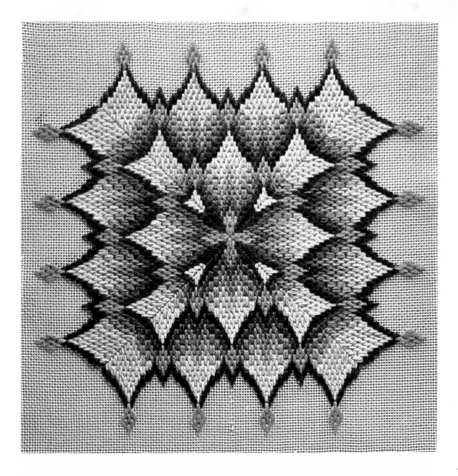

Plate 10

Plate 11

Plate 12

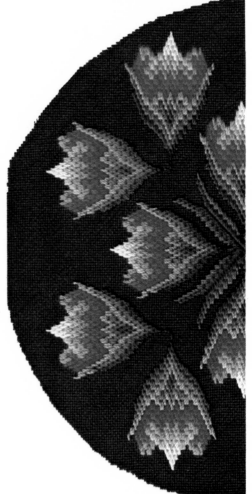

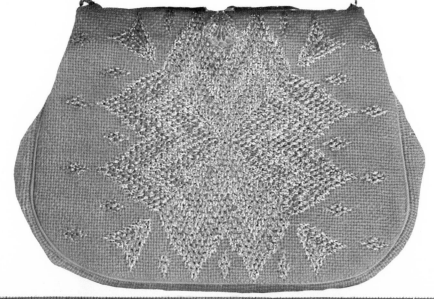

Plate 13

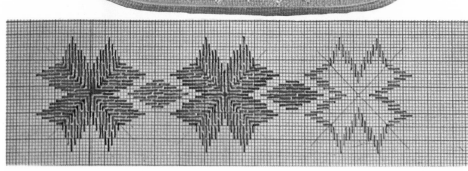

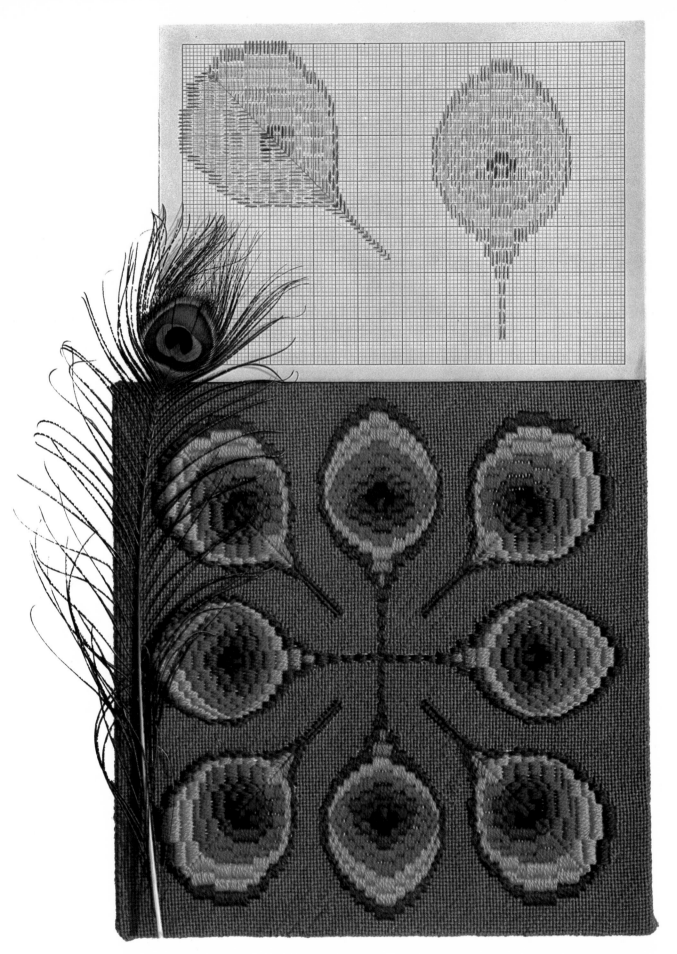

Plate 14

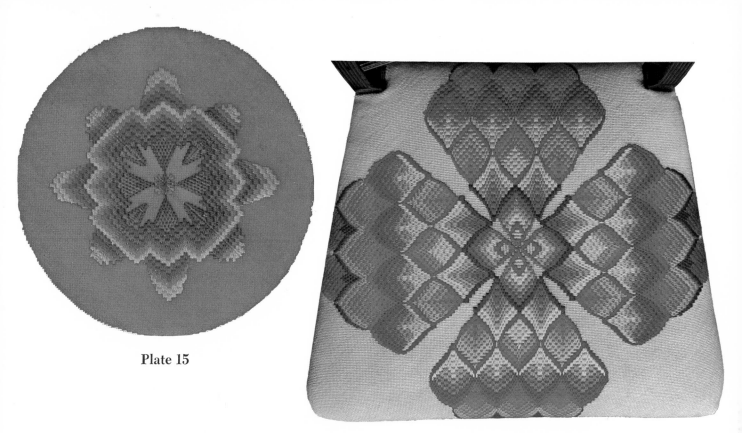

Plate 15

Plate 17

Plate 16

Plate 18

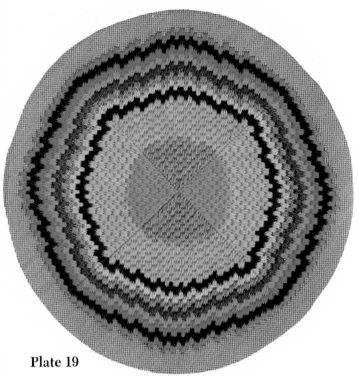

Plate 19

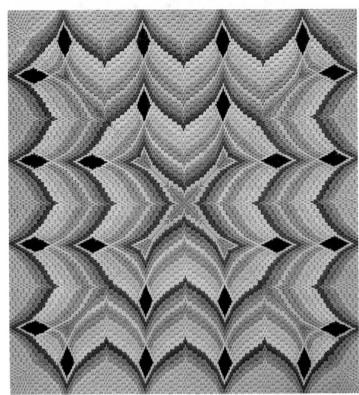

Plate 21

Plate 20

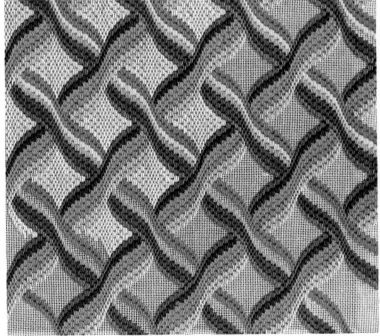

Plate 22

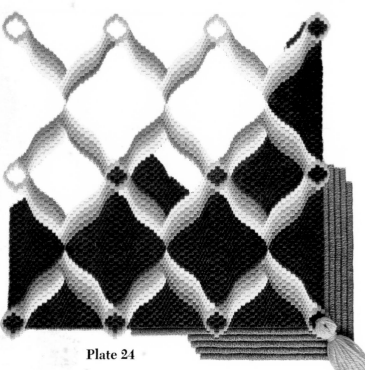

Plate 23

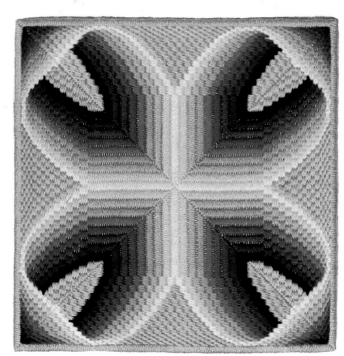

Plate 25

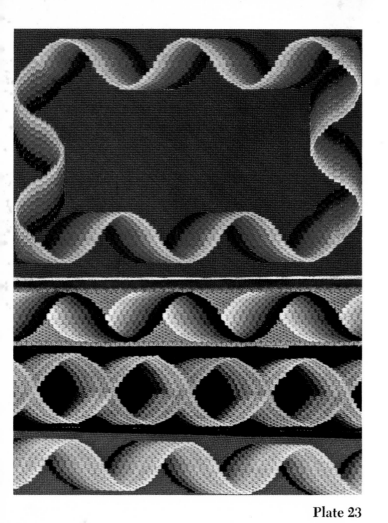

Plate 24

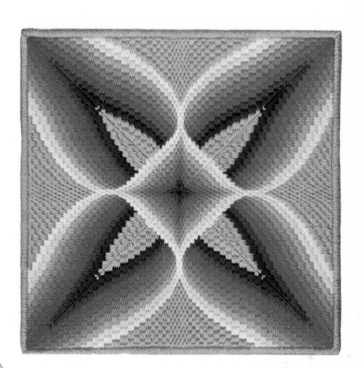

Plate 26

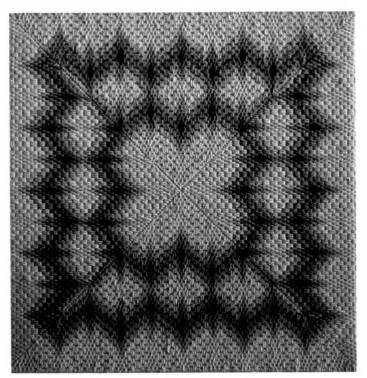

Plate 27

Plate 29

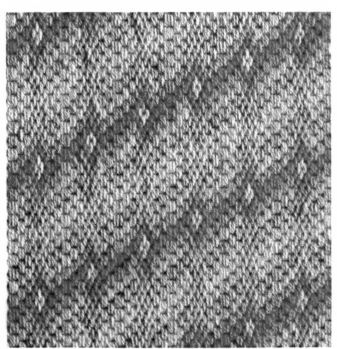

Plate 28

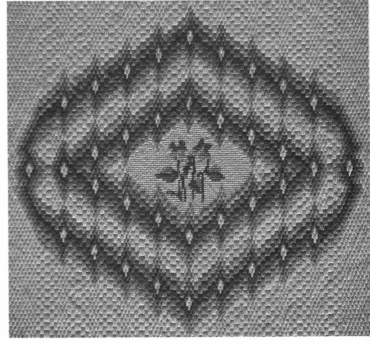

Plate 30

Plate 31

Plate 32

Plate 33

Plate 34

This lovely border was designed by Mrs. Richard Sanders. She used five shades of taupe Persian dark to light 110, 114, 583, 134, 136. Background 843. 14 mesh, 3 strands, background tent stitch, 2 strands.

Taupe border, burnt orange background

Peacock feathers   This pattern could be worked differently; for example, I would like to see the center feathers started 5 stitches away from the center. This should give a rounder look to the design rather than a square. Another way would be to work the feathers in one direction only. If worked as charted, the measurements would be as follows: 18 mesh—17″ diameter, 14 mesh—21″ diameter, 12 mesh—24″ diameter, 10 mesh—30″ diameter. So on the 10 mesh canvas it would make a lovely round rug. (opposite)

The worked piece shown in color plate 14 is 14 mesh canvas, Persian colors. Dark olive 583, mauve 229, chartreuse 550 (Persian crewel, cinnamon 422), turquoise 718, navy 321, royal 723. Background 553.

Leaf stitch   I first worked out the leaf stitch in the four way method on a sampler of stitches. On the sampler I had three side stitches on each leaf before the tapering (as the stitch is shown in Hope Hanley's book, *Needlepoint*). When I started the large piece below, I wondered why my corners were different

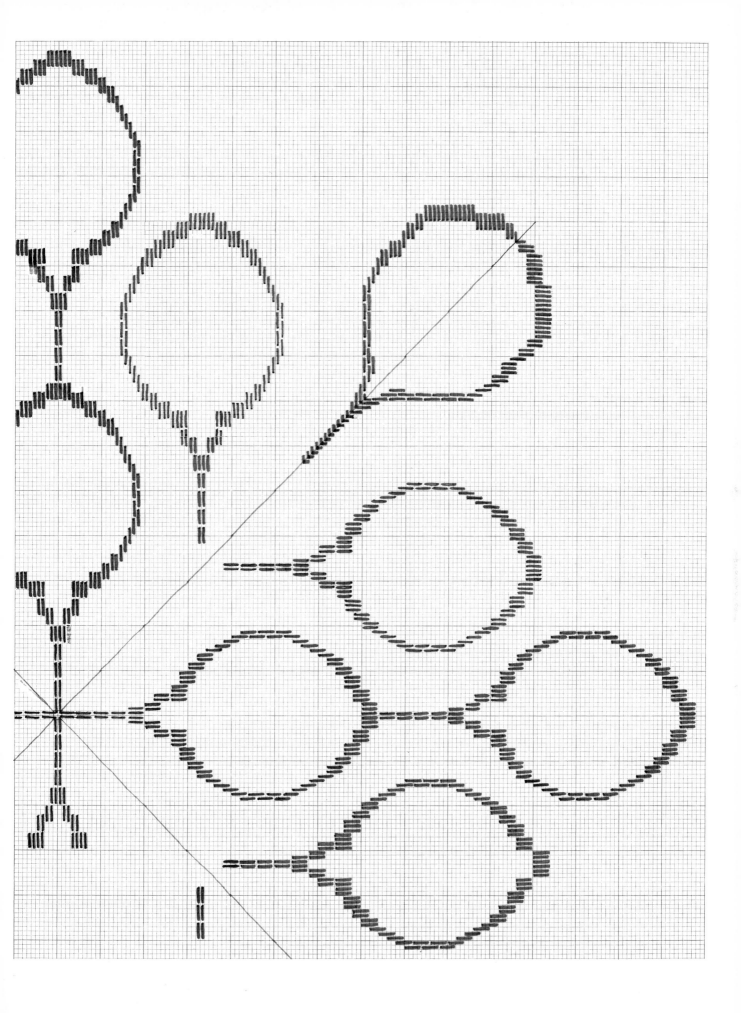

and I ripped out the work several times until I discovered I had four side stitches which enlarged my leaves and of course my corners would not meet at the same time the smaller ones did. Mrs. Samuel F. Pierson of Stamford did the pillow at left using just the center square of three shades as a spaced repeat. We both used 10 mesh, 3 strands Persian. My colors are greens, dark to light 569, 579, 589. Background 738. Mrs. Pierson's colors are blue, dark to light 365, 330, 386, rose 282, background 440. She also used the brick stitch to complete her background.

The chart below shows how to do the leaf stitch with three side stitches and with four side stitches. It also shows part of the repeat pattern for Mrs. Pierson's design. The 3rd row of leaf stitches meet at the corners. My design does not meet until the 4th row of leaf stitches.

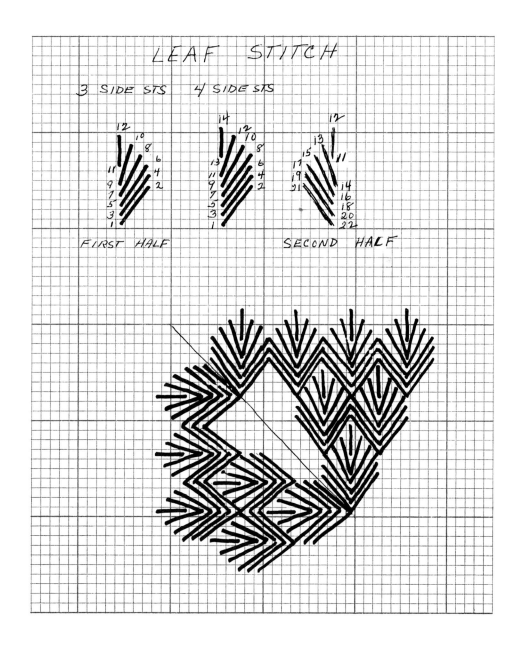

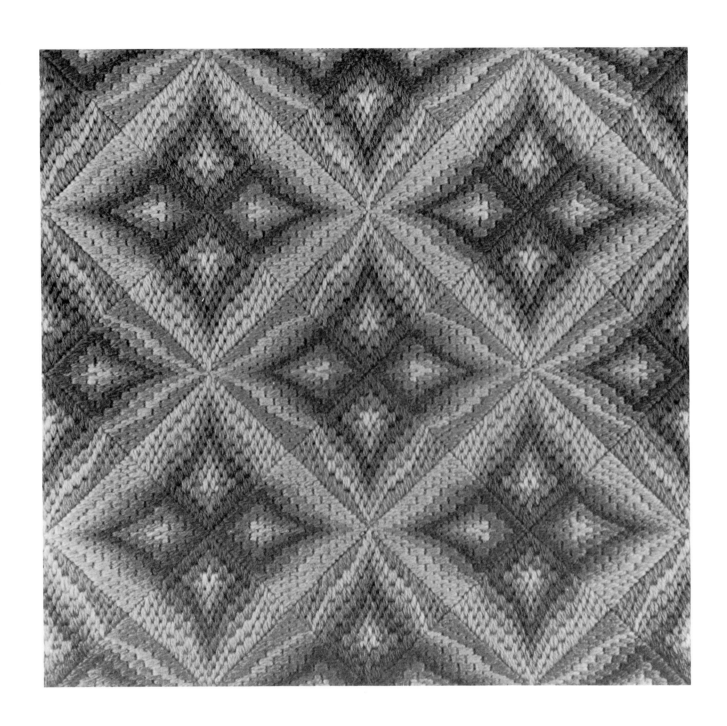

Green blocks with shocking pink This piece designed by Mrs. Sanders is very fresh with its green and shocking pinks. The four shades of green Persian dark to light are G54, G64, 574, and G74. The shocking pinks are 827 and 828. 14 mesh, 3 strands.

One of my students asked me to do a border design for a circular piece. The soft olive and turquoise border worked out quite easily. I drew a circle and miter lines on graph paper and then with the 4-2 step did the outside ring first. When stitching the design on canvas it was easy to work from the outside toward the center. (I counted out from the center so as to know where to begin.) The stripes could have been repeated all the way to the center, but I decided to use a melon background and then do the quartered circle in the middle. Persian yarn dark to light. Green 540, 553, 590, 593, turquoise 728, 748. Background 978. 12 mesh, 3 strands. This is also shown in color in plate 19.

Soft green and turquoise on melon

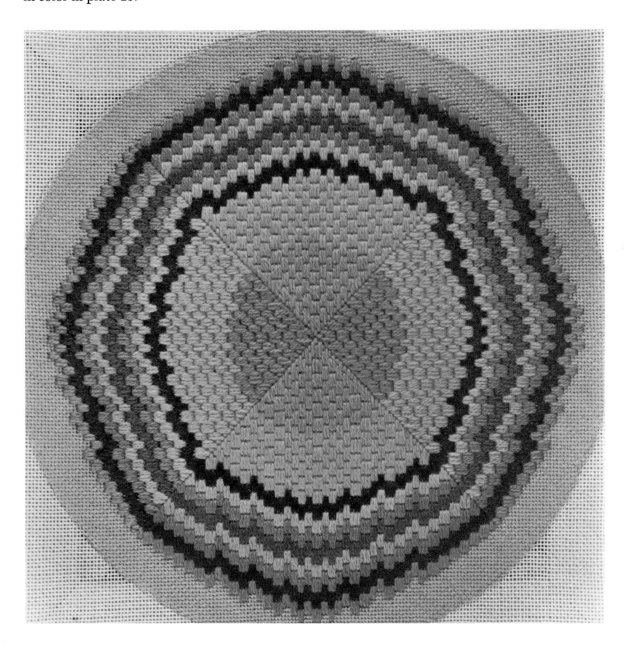

Red and blue circles   The center quartered circle of the previous design gave me the idea to go on to the red and blue circles in a repeat. This gives an op-art effect. When the white background was worked, phantom squares appeared. Persian yarn red R10, blue 723, white 005. 14 mesh, 3 strands. The chart on facing page shows the outer row of the circle only. The above is a detail of the complete design as shown.

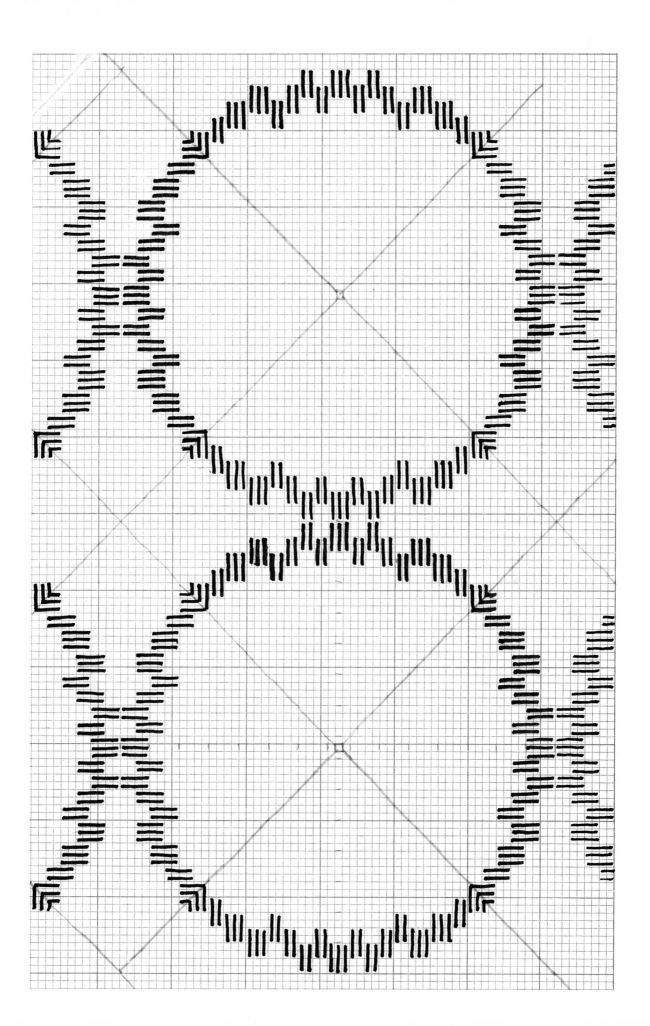

This is an adaptation of a design I made up some time ago. The color plate 18 shows how you can separate sections of the design with background between. There could be only one row between or as many as you choose. The color between could also be shaded. The chart at left shows the main outline of the design as in the worked piece, A and also with the second row of design attached to the first row, B. Persian colors dark to light. Blue 723, 731, 741, Bg. 756, Green 559, 550. 12 mesh, 3 strands.

Emerald and sapphire center and border

In this small pattern I shaded the greens in the usual manner, but did the brown shading from side to side. It would look quite different if the browns were shaded in the same direction as the greens. Other patterns could be done this way. Persian colors dark to light. Brown 120, 145, 462, 466, 492. Green 545, 550, 565, 580, Bg. 580. Gold outline 521. 14 mesh, 3 strands. This shows just the center of the final piece which is considerably larger.

Earthy browns and greens

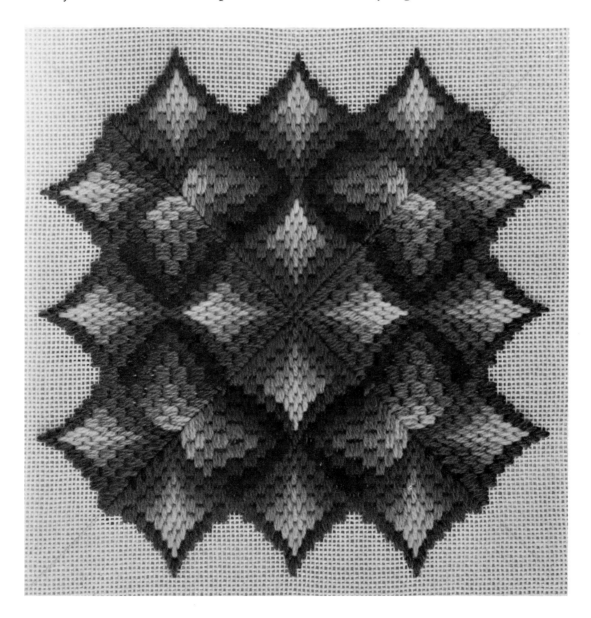

Gold shields
on teal

This design as shown in color plate 21 and this chart was worked on 16 mesh with Nantucket golds from dark to light 11, 8, 9, two rows of each. The very dark diamond centers are teal 71. The other teal shades are from dark to light, Nantucket 70, Persian 773 and 783, Nantucket 107. Nantucket yarns were used as it comes (4 strands), Persian yarns 2 strands. The dark diamonds were filled in with a diamond stitch as shown in the small chart. Of course, it could be done in Bargello. It was just fun to have a little variation. On the 16 mesh canvas the center set of shields and diamonds measures 10″ across. If this was worked on 10 mesh this same amount of design would measure close to 16″. The diamond stitch shown in the chart is based on the leaf stitch. (There are 7 stitches from each side crowded into the center hole of the diamond).

A Group of Ribbons

Ribbon candy border

When working out the ribbon candy to turn a corner, I did only one corner on graph paper, then figured the number of canvas threads needed to make a rectangle and meet. I did the first row of the lightest color which came out perfectly. Then, when I put my second color in, I found that in every other corner the "ribbon" flipped over so that the alternate corners are different. If you want to make all four corners the same you would have to change the shading at the centers of the side edges. Then the ribbon would not have a continuous ripple. If you shade toward the outside as partially shown in the chart, you will have the pointed corners. 12 mesh canvas, Persian colors dark to light 201, 236, 240, 242, 843, 852, 853, 870, Background 723. 3 strands for design and background. Color plate 23 shows this piece and the 3 following designs.

Ribbon candy border chart

I used both corners 1 and 2 and the B side of the chart for my ribbon candy border. If you use only corner 1 and A side of the chart all four corners will be alike.

Blue, green ribbon

This was the first ribbon that I did and I used the darkest color to set up the pattern. When I did the other ribbon designs, I used the lightest color for this first row. It works better using the light color if you wish to give the feeling of depth. The Persian colors in order are blue 365, 740, aqua 773, 718, 728, 738, 748, green 589, G37, white 005, background 579 worked in the Bargello with the Scotch stitch border alternating the direction of each square. 12 mesh, 3 strands. See plate 23.

66

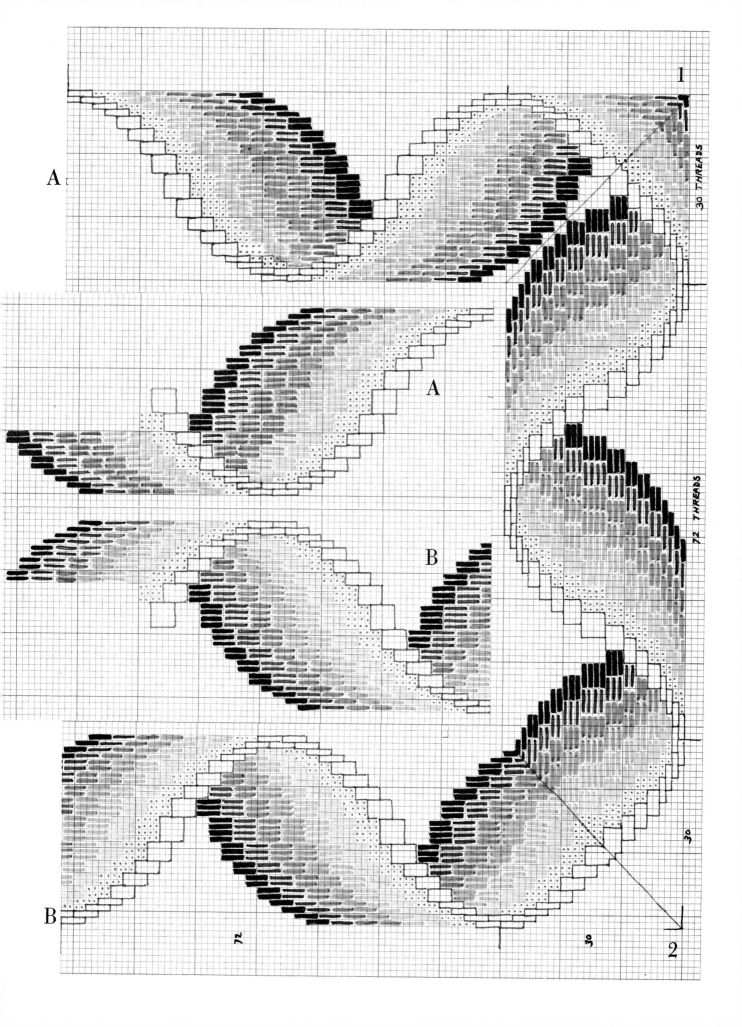

Yellow, orange ribbon 12 mesh, 3 strands. Persian colors light to dark, 040, 468, 456, 457, 447, 427, 433, 511. Background 424 in tent stitch, also 3 strands. See plate 23.

Green double ribbon 12 mesh 3 strands. Persian color blue-greens 524, 526, 579, 589, 566, G37. Yellow-greens 545, 574, 550, G74, 570, 575. Background 528 in tent stitch, also 3 strands. See plate 23.

Woven ribbons Plate 22 shows the worked piece as having 7 stitches in the width of the ribbons and the chart below shows them with only 5 stitches wide. They can be made either wider or narrower. In the finished piece I have used some single rows of a color and also double rows of a color. I did not stay with one family of shading in each ribbon. However, you could certainly work them in shades of one color. The ribbons weaving from right to left are in greens. The color numbers from right to left are Nantucket yarns 84, 78, 83, 82 and 77. The ribbons weaving from left to right are blues and turquoise. Colors from left to right are Nantucket's 58 and 59, Persian 738, Nantucket's 70 and 60. The background is Nantucket's pale blue 53. This was worked on 16 mesh using Nantucket yarn as it comes and 2 strands of the Persian.

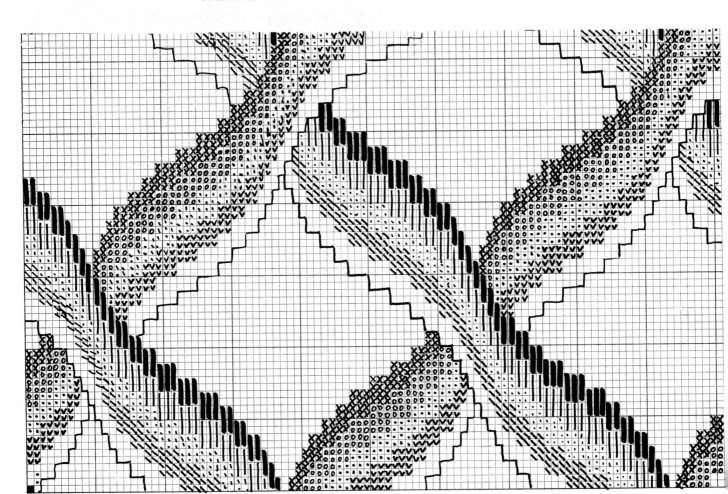

I am going to use the ribbon variation shown in plate 24 as a pillow in my library. The ribbon colors from dark to light are Persian 545, 550, 446, 580, 040. The middle color, 446, was used instead of 565, which is part of that family, because it's a strong greenish yellow which I need in order to pick up the colors of my sofa. The wallpaper in this room is a yellow caning pattern on white so that this design goes quite well with it.

Yellow green twisted ribbons and rings

In setting up this design I used the middle color as the dominant line and also used it for the rings. The chart on page 70 shows the rings as another color. The unworked background section as seen in the color plate shows how a white background would look. In the finished section I've used a very dark background 540 olive green so as to make the ribbons show up more dramatically. The border is done in a very simple four way Bargello using color number 553, a lighter olive. I'll stitch tassels to the remaining corners as I have to the center of the ring at the finished corner.

This was worked on 16 mesh using 2 strands. Each motif measures 4½″ x 6″. On a 10 mesh canvas the motifs would measure 6½″ x 9″ and would be bold enough for a rug.

The charts on page 71 show variations of this design. The top chart shows it in outline form without being folded or shaded, but progressing at a slight diagonal as in the finished piece shown in photo below.

Red folded ribbons and rings

The bottom chart shows rounder rings touching each other instead of being spaced apart. They are also on the same level with each other which makes each side of the ribbons equal. A shows the shading from dark to light using four shades and repeating this for each ribbon. B shows two ribbons shading from dark at the edges to light centers, using three shades. The next ribbon is left as another color, then the next 2 ribbons are shaded like the first two.

You can make the rings a different color—there could be several colors in the ribbons; one in shades of green, the next in shades of gold, etc. This design should be suitable for valance boards, a headboard and waste-baskets.

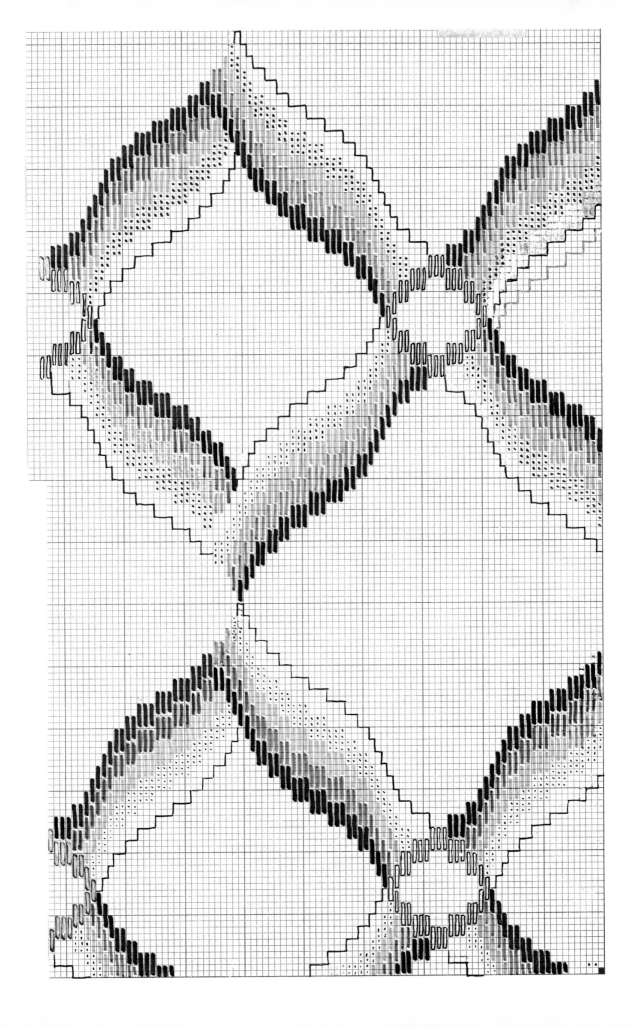

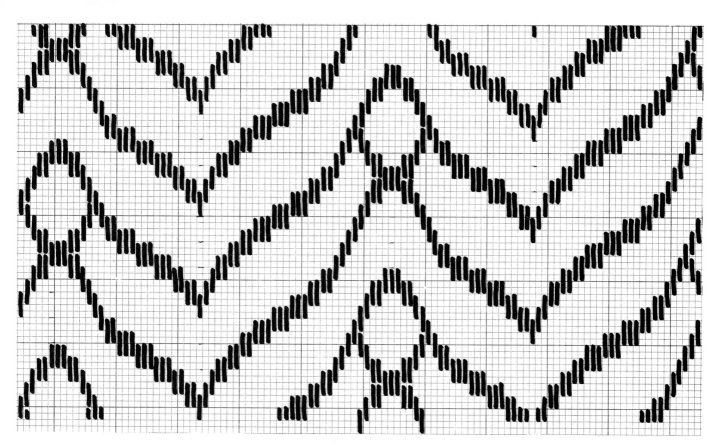

A

B

The finished piece was worked on 16 mesh using Nantucket yarn just as it comes. This yarn covers the 16 mesh beautifully. The colors used were reds from dark to light, 33, 32, 31, 30, 29. The background is white no. 1.

Mauve ribbon corners

When making the chart for the ribbon candy border, I kept wondering what would happen if I used the pointed corner section as a four corner repeat. In the mauve piece I modified it a little and put the "folded over" corners to the outside and allowed the main row of the design to meet at the center. Then the remaining shades joined at the miters. In this design, I did use a single thread stitch at the miters, keeping it a bit loose so as not to lose it. This design has 9 shades as shown in color plate 25, which gives it great depth. Persian yarn dark to light. Navy 321, purple 610, 891, 228, 227, the next shade is one I had dyed with lichens, 229, 256, pink 837. Background 652, 12 mesh, 3 strands.

The lichen used for this color is *Umbilicaria Pustulata*. I gathered some of these lichens a few years ago along the coast of Maine. We found them on a foggy day on large rocks by a hill and they looked like dark olive-green pieces of kelp. I found the recipe in *Lichens for Vegetable Dyeing by* Eileen M. Bolton.

After doing the mauve piece I decided to turn the corners around to have them meet at the center. This looks entirely different. The corners become a central motif. If a couple of background stitches separated the four designs instead of allowing them to meet, I think the effect would be different again. Persian yarn dark to light, rust 266, 215, orange 958, 960, 965, 970, 975, yellow 467, 438. Background 565. 12 mesh, 3 strands. See color plate 26.

Orange ribbon corners

Various Ways of
Using a Design

The color plates 27 thru 30 show how a design can be done as regular Bargello, four way Bargello, worked on a diagonal or turned into a diamond border. It might be fun to try this with other patterns. You will find that some will work and some will not.

Four way border in soft blues This design first started as a regular Bargello piece as shown in chart on facing page, in oranges as a sample for a headboard. I thought the design had many possibilities, which you will see. In this border design, I used 4 shades of blue. The chart on page 76 shows the four way version. The darkest blue 365 was used for the small diamond centers, then dark to light —330, 385, 386. The background is B43, a very pale blue. This is a 12 mesh canvas using 3 strands of yarn.

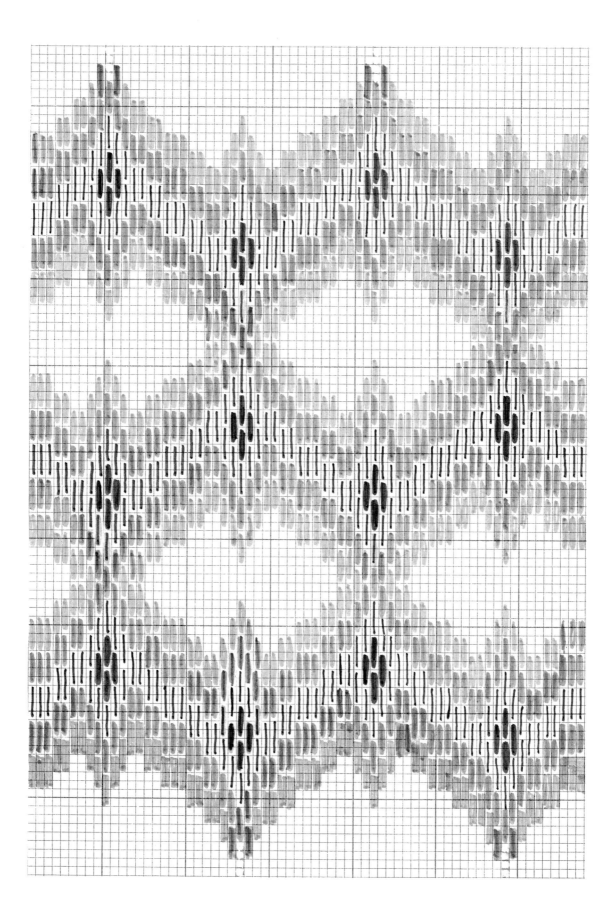

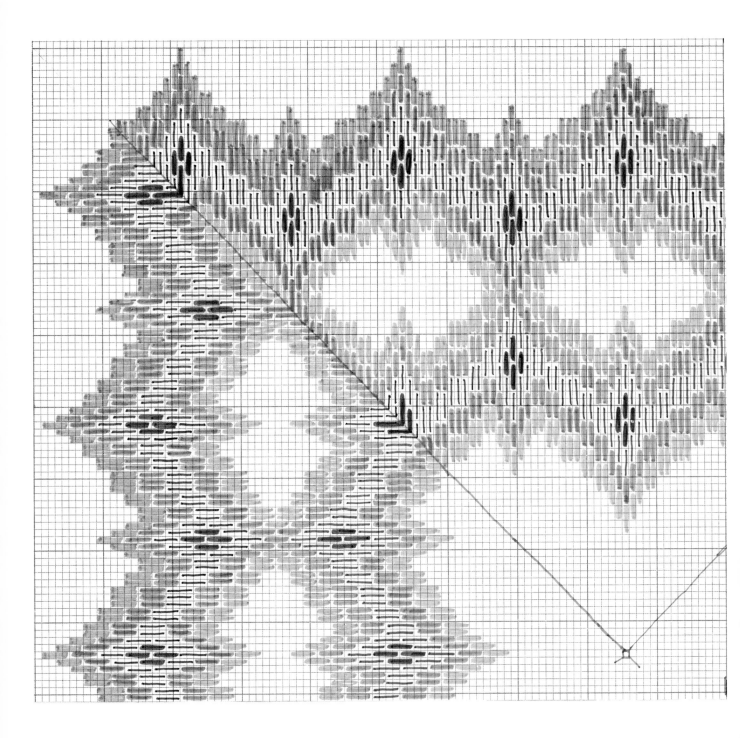

This is the same basic design worked in the regular way. The center of the small diamonds is color 506, then the other greens dark to light are 505, 510, 555, 570, 575. After finishing all the greens, I decided to fill the remaining spaces with gold. Notice in the chart below that the gold shading is done in a serpentine manner. On one row of openings the shading is done from the left and the next row is done from the right. The golds from dark to light are 511, 521, 531, 541, 455, 438, 468; off white is 012.

Regular Bargello in greens and golds

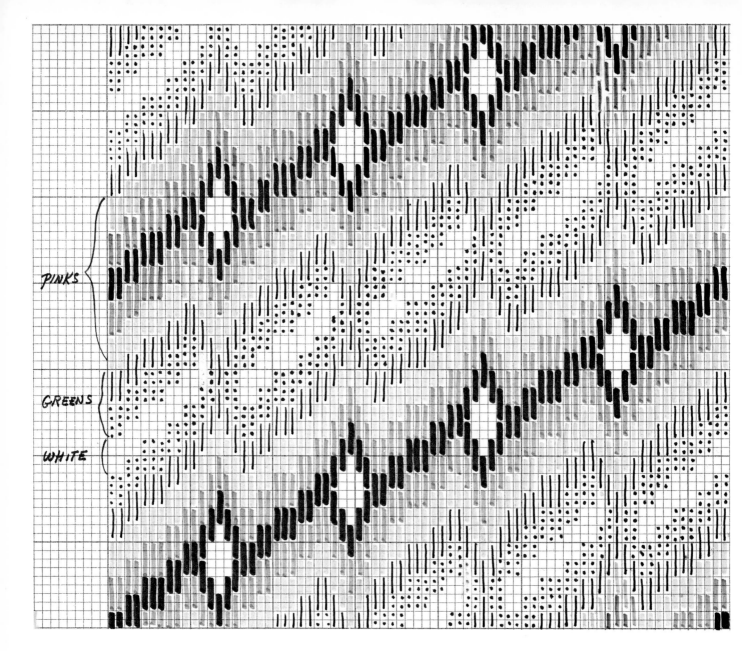

PINKS

GREENS

WHITE

Diagonal in pinks and greens	The same basic design was worked in a diagonal way this time. The pinks from dark to light are 850, 860, 870. The greens are 589, G37, and white 005.
The Diagonal re-worked into a Diamond	After working the diagonal design, I tried reversing the direction. This worked out very well as a diamond-shaped border. Then I decided to put small flowers in the center (in this case violets). Blues, dark to light, 611, 621, 631, 641; pink background 831. The greens in the leaves are dark to light 505, 510, 555. Various flowers could be used in the center as well as a monogram.

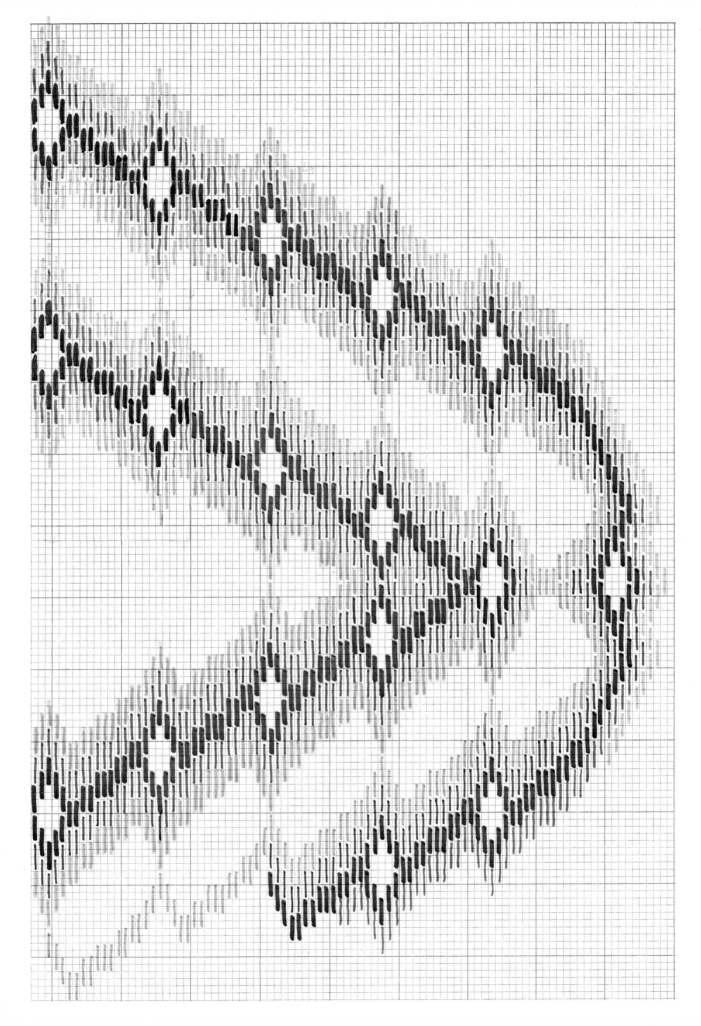

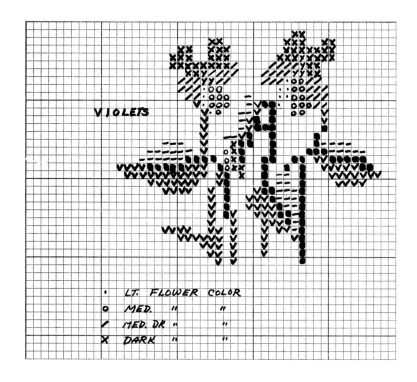

VIOLETS

• LT. FLOWER COLOR
○ MED. " "
/ MED. DK " "
X DARK " "

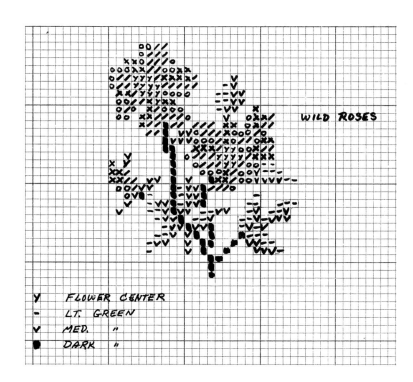

WILD ROSES

Y FLOWER CENTER
- LT. GREEN
V MED. "
● DARK "

Needlepoint Pieces

58″ x 58″ Rug This rug, shown at right, was a challenge. I had wanted to do one for some time. I also wanted to find out if a piece of this size could be carried to meetings—it was not difficult at all to take it with me.

I worked the first few motifs out on graph paper then went to work right on the canvas which is 10 mesh mono, 5′ wide. I cut a length of 1⅔ yds. so as to be sure of having enough for hems. 5 strands of Persian yarn was used. The first round of motifs, starting at the center, was from black to white; 050, 108, 162, 164, 166, 147, 017, 005. The next round of motifs started with the black outline (which, incidentally, was used throughout), then dark brown 110, dk. gold brown 131, dark taupe 583, medium taupe 573, medium gold 479, light taupe 563, pale taupe 015, off white 012. The background is gold 433.

I kept count of some of the quantities used, as follows: Black ¼ lb., dark brown ¼ lb. + 5 strands, dark gold brown ¼ lb. + 22 strands, dark taupe ¼ lb. + 2 small skeins, med. taupe ¼ lb. + 4 strands, med. gold approx. ¼ lb., light taupe, ¼ lb., pale taupe approx,. ¼ lb., off white approx. ¼ lb., white 6 oz., background 1¼ lbs. plus a small amount.

I worked 2 rows of tent stitch around entire rug so that when it was hemmed for finishing the canvas would be less apt to show.

This rug took approximately 5½ weeks to stitch, working 8 to 12 hours a day, almost 7 days a week.

The chart for this rug is on the next 4 pages.

After blocking the rug, it was finished by turning in approximately 1″ of canvas and stitching to the wrong side. Rabbit skin glue was used to size the back—this also helps to keep the rug in shape. Then a piece of canvas was blind stitched to the back of the rug for a lining.

82

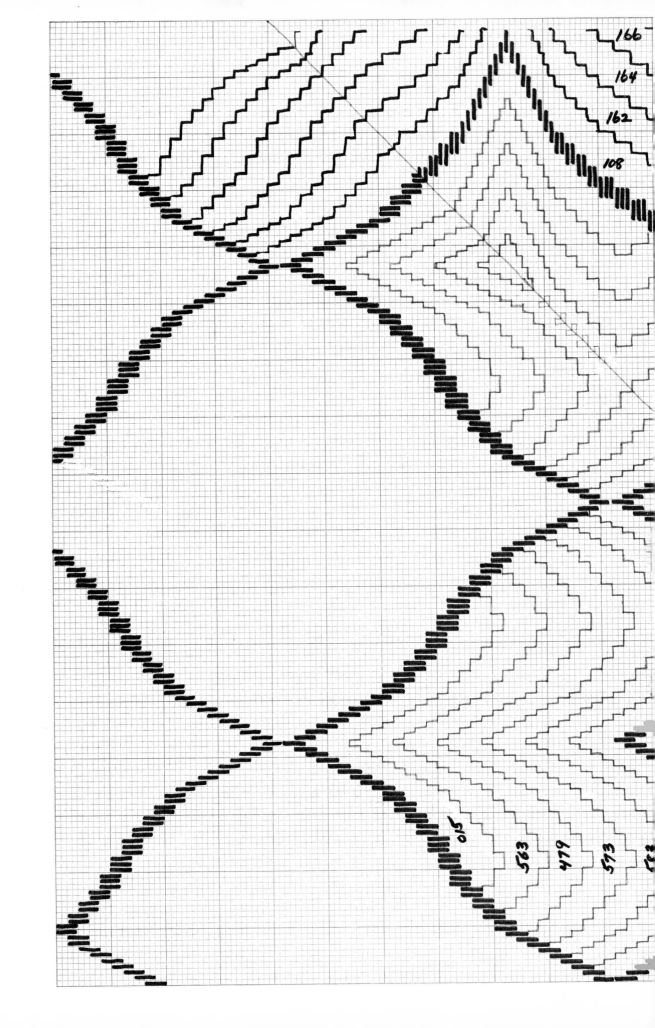

2 ROWS OF EACH SHADE

131

110

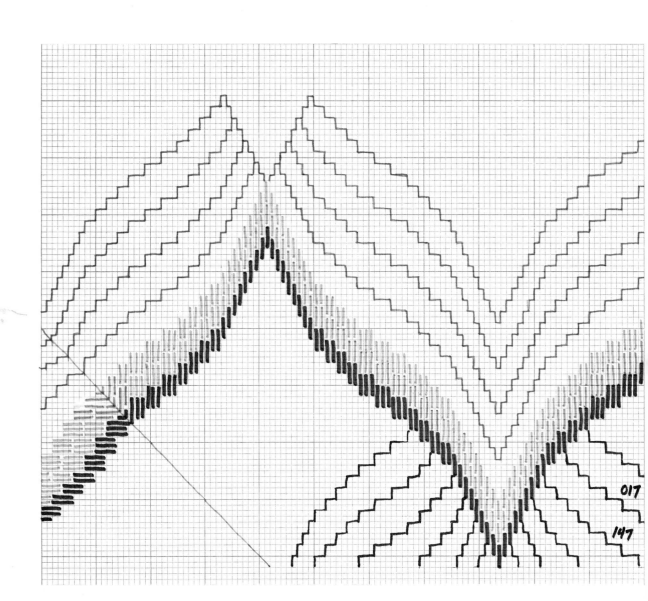

017

147

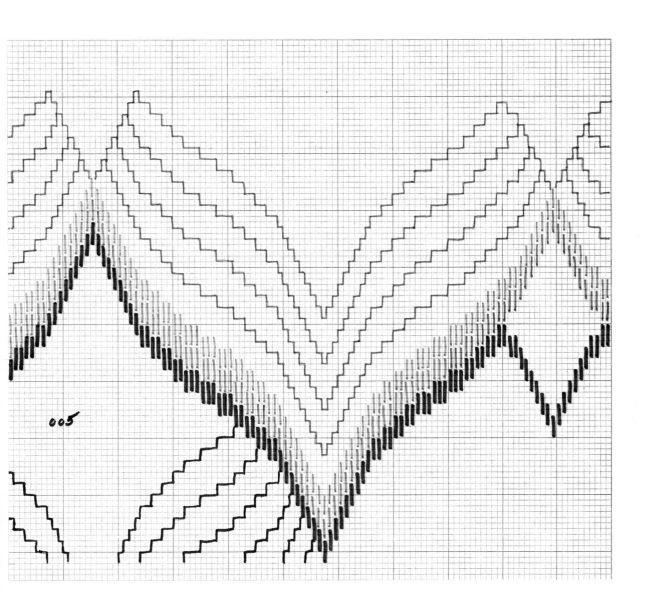

005

Plate 31 shows 2 different color renditions of the same fern design. The pink and green on the bamboo chair was done by Mrs. Ogden K. Myers of Darien. The all-green ferns is mine. Mrs. George Park of Stamford stitched the two arm chairs for me and Mrs. Walter Hafner of Darien stitched the four side chairs. It's nice to have friends like this. The green one won the first award in needlepoint chairs in the West Hartford Needlework show in October, 1970.

The floral bench was worked for me by Mrs. Hafner. I designed this piece to take with me on a trip, but didn't get much done, so my friend took it over to finish and now I'm enjoying it in my living room.

Plate 32 shows a paisley rug which was designed to fit the front entrance hall of the Charles Faggs in Darien. Their house had just been redecorated and a paisley print with these colors was used for draperies. The rug is 44″ x 89½″ and was worked in one piece on 8 mesh penelope canvas.

The first piece of needlepoint I ever designed for Mrs. Fagg was the first of three panels for a folding screen, about twenty years ago. She has since finished the other two panels. I was able to match the background color in weaving yarns and wove the material for the other side of the screen.

Plate 33 shows a couple of pillows. The daisy has a double cross stitch center (70 in Hope Hanley's *Needlepoint*) and a turkey stitch bee. This pillow has encouraged a number of others to use assorted stitches in their needle-point pieces.

The "paperweight" pillow I did as a Christmas present for friends who have a lovely collection of antique and modern glass paperweights. This is an adaptation of one of the lovely overlays. I've seen it worked in several color combinations. Since designing this pillow, I've done many coasters using an assortment of paperweight designs, also other pillows.

Plate 34 shows the stair risers (treads are folded under so as to be able to photograph) which I designed for our stairs. We've worn out the stair carpeting that I had woven some years ago, so decided to do some in needlepoint. I feel that the needlepoint will hold up better, but if it does start to wear, I can restitch the worn places before the canvas goes.

George and I love nature's flowers and creatures. The wild flowers grow in our woods and gardens and every once in a while we see a toad in the garden—and not far from us are frogs and skunk cabbage. One day George was at the work bench in the garage and turned around to see a little deer mouse sitting on the windowsill washing its face. The chipmunks are all around us and when we put sunflower seeds on the terrace one will come up and scoop them up like a little vacuum cleaner till his cheeks bulge, then he takes them home and comes back for more.

The next step is "Buffy." When our house was being built we used to stop by every morning on the way to business and again on the way home. For a while we noticed a cat was around and getting more and more hungry. When she ate two slices of bread one evening we realized that she had been dropped off by someone. The next morning we brought her milk and food and I made the remark that if we had to have another cat, I wished it would be a red one. Two days later she brought in "Buffy," the cutest little red kitten. We fed them together for a few days, then took Buffy with us each evening and back to her mother mornings until a neighbor took the mother. We had Buffy for fifteen years until one night she disappeared and we haven't seen her since. We keep wondering what happened to her.

The rabbits have frustrated me in my vegetable garden—eating off the green beans as fast as they would grow new leaves, also the young peas. Finally we fenced in the vegetable garden, but we still see them around and in the raspberries which we share with them and all the birds.

Next is "Crafty." He was brought to us when George was ill. He didn't like cats, either—at that time. This one won him over and was a real character and a gentleman. We named him after our business (The Handcraft Shoppe) and the name suited him. He, too, was with us for fifteen years until he became ill and had to leave us.

The top riser is one of the pheasants and brood which are around. One day we watched a father pheasant and six young on our side of the road. Father was trying to get all six to the other side—five went willingly but the sixth kept balking and was frightened to walk across. Finally, he got up nerve to fly across.

We see possums, skunks and raccoons and many birds but have run out of steps on which to represent them.

The fern at each side of the risers continues on the treads. The rug at the top of the stairs in the hall has a border of the ferns and a repeat of small fern fiddles in the center.

The canvas used was 5 mesh penelope. We used 9 strands of Persian yarn for the background, working in the large holes only, but the designs were done with 3 strands using every hole so as to get the detail.

Mrs. Park helped me with the stair pieces and she stitched the entire hall rug.

Yarns Used For The Designs In This Book

Paternayan Bros. Inc.
312 East 95th St.   *Persian yarn*
New York, N. Y. 10028

Nantucket Needleworks
11 South Water St.   *Persian type yarn*
Nantucket, Mass. 02554

Handwork Tapestries
3389 Colony Drive   *New Zealand yarn*
Baldwin, N.Y. 11510   *from France*

Other Sources Of Persian Type Yarn

Bernard Ulmann Co.
30-20 Thomson Ave.
Long Island City, N.Y. 11101

Paragon Art Needlework
385 Fifth Ave.
New York, N.Y.

Reynolds International Needlework Guild, Inc.
215 Central Avenue
East Farmingdale, N.Y. 11735

Columbia-Minerva Corp.
295 Fifth Avenue
New York, N.Y. 10016

Brunswick Worsted Mills, Inc.
Moosup, Conn. 06354

Scovill Manufacturing Co.
Box 5028
Spartanburg, S.C.

Spinnerin Yarn Co., Inc.
230 Fifth Ave.
New York, N.Y.

Craft Yarns of R.I., Inc.
603 Mineral Spring Ave.
Pawtucket, R. I. 02862

Bibliography

Hope Hanley *Needlepoint* Charles Scribner's Sons, N.Y. 1964

Maggie Lane *Needlepoint by Design* Charles Scribner's Sons, N.Y. 1970

Barbara Snook *Florentine Embroidery* Charles Scribner's Sons, 1967

Elsa S. Williams *Bargello* Van Nostrand Reinhold Co., N.Y. 1967

Eileen M. Bolton *Lichens For Vegetable Dyeing* Charles T. Brandford Company, Newton Centre, Mass. 1960

NOTES

NOTES

NOTES

NOTES

NOTES